FOR
WRITERS
ONLY

Also by Sophy Burnham

FOR WRITERS ONLY

Sophy
Burnham

BALLANTINE BOOKS · NEW YORK

All rights reserved under International
and Pan-American Copyright Conventions. Published
in the United States by Ballantine Books, a division of Random
House, Inc., New York, and simultaneously in Canada
by Random House of Canada Limited, Toronto.

Grateful acknowledgment is made
to New Directions Publishing Corporation
and David Higham Associates Limited for permission
to reprint "In My Craft or Sullen Art" from *The Poems of
Dylan Thomas*, published in the United States by New Directions
Publishing Corp. and in Great Britain by Dent. Copyright
© 1946 by New Directions Publishing Corp. Reprinted
by permission of New Directions Publishing Corp.
and David Higham Associates Ltd.

LIBRARY OF CONGRESS CATALOGING-IN-PUBLICATION DATA
Burnham, Sophy.
    For writers only / Sophy Burnham.
        p.   cm.
    ISBN 0-345-37317-0
    1. Authorship—Anecdotes. 2. Authorship—Quotations,
maxims, etc.   I. Title.
PN165.B87   1994
808'.02—dc20   94-13765
                                                CIP

Text design by Holly Johnson

Manufactured in the United States of America

First Edition: November 1994

10 9 8 7 6 5 4 3 2 1

In my craft or sullen art
Exercised in the still night
When only the moon rages
And the lovers lie abed
With all their griefs in their arms,
I labour by singing light
Not for ambition or bread
Or the strut and trade of charms
On the ivory stages
But for the common wages
Of their most secret heart.

Not for the proud man apart
From the raging moon I write
On these spindrift pages
Nor for the towering dead
With their nightingales and psalms
But for the lovers, their arms
Round the griefs of the ages
Who pay no praise or wages
Nor heed my craft or art.

DYLAN THOMAS

CONTENTS

PREFACE

Last night I dreamt I was leading a huge bay draft horse as long as a locomotive. It had enormous dark brown and expressive eyes. Its name was Simenon. William Styron (whom I have never met but whose work I admire) was to ride this horse, and over my shoulder I could see him leading up my own white shaggy rough little Shetland pony. Which says everything about my credentials to write this book—I, the Sancho Panza to the Dons.

Wasn't it H. L. Mencken who said he would be remembered only as a footnote in literary history, like one of the calming little ponies that walk the thoroughbred racehorses from the stable out to the track? As I get older, this pony-status sometimes seems okay.

This book was written for myself at a time when my career as a writer had come almost to a halt. I felt lost. Not that I had stopped writing; no, I rose every morning and worked, sometimes feverishly all day. In eight years, I wrote six books as well as short stories, essays, articles, plays. . . . The problem lay not in the writing but in the lack of acknowledgment and support. I didn't want to write what people would pay me to write, and no one wanted to pay me for what I wanted to write.

I cried a lot.

I fought myself.

I fell prey to Fear and to the inner Judge whose name is Doubt—or Self-abuse!

Sometimes I couldn't write at all.

I started this book, then, as a means of encouraging myself in the lonely days of creating, while still picking out the path. When desperate, I could open it at any page and read a few paragraphs, forward or backward—it doesn't matter—and close the manuscript, ready again to face my real work: telling stories; trying, in the words of Tacitus, "to touch the minds and hearts of Man."

You will notice here my fascination with the nineteenth-century writers, English, French and Russian. That is because these were the heroes I grew up with. These are the ones to hold up for me a guiding light, for these are the ones who have survived longer than their lifetimes or longer than a few media-boosted years. And these are the ones—especially the women—of whom I could say, "If *she* could create, faced with social prejudice and poverty, how dare I make excuses for myself!"

You will also find an occasional reference to a painter or musician or sculptor. I'm told they have no place in a work for writers, but I disagree. It brings me comfort, knowing that all artists suffer the same emotions, failings, and struggles to pursue their craft. Their experiences have given me heart when I didn't have another ounce of strength. And so I pass them on.

Since this book was written for myself, the first person singular hardly appeared in its early draft; it was not I who interested me but other writers—the Masters! How did they work? What tricks did they use to seduce the Muse or cope with interruptions? Parry fear?

Ironically, in recent years, my work has unexpectedly received attention—all those unwanted words that I spent years upon!—and now my editor asks me to insert more of myself into the book. My first impulse is to refuse. I shy back, a little embarrassed at placing myself in the ranks of "real writers" (although my whole life has been an attempt to earn that name). But vanity sneaks onto the playing field as well, and pride, and also pleasure at sharing what I've learned in thirty years; and soon I know my confidence will increase. Soon my editor may regret ever opening that faucet, for it will all come pouring out, the tedious history of another writer in love with words, another writer fighting herself, the words, the confusions and obfuscations of her own mind in an effort to be clear, fighting the very conditions that are necessary to the writing itself.

Already the book is changing shape. I reread it and like Tolstoy see *it doesn't do at all; it must be rewritten, all of it.*

⊗

This book gives no advice on how to write, on tone or technique or style. It's about the emotions you go through when working. To this degree *For Writers Only* isn't only for writers: it applies as much to a carpenter or composer as to a writer, for the passions of creation are always the same, and probably The Creator Itself, the Loving One, felt similar exhilaration and despair when first fashioning the world all those six long days ago. Therefore, don't look to this book to teach you writing tricks or how to find an agent or meet the publisher who'll love your work. This is about the sweetness of creating instead.

You read your draft—and want to slash your wrists.

Well, that is the appropriate emotion to feel. Wait. Tomorrow you'll begin another phase.

Even as I write these words, I'm aware of uneasiness, of anxiety swirling darkly in me; for each time I begin I am a neophyte, as if never having written a word before. The only difference is that I've traveled this way before. I recognize the landmarks now—that dreadful mountain rearing up, the chasm yawning at my feet, that lambent valley. I recognize the winding path, even over stony places where no prints show. "Oh yes," I say. "The sheer-terror-at-beginning phase. I've been here before." And I know that tomorrow, or next week, the landscape will be different. It may be foggy and rainy—or glorious!—but it will not be the same.

❈

I give this book, then, to all writers, to all creative people, to all of us poor troubled humans who are struggling with our doubts and love. I hope that it will live in your hands until it drops, stained and dog-eared, into dust, too yellowed and frayed even for the outdoor racks of second-hand bookstores. I hope you steal it from libraries and buy it in stores to give to your sons or wives or daughters or nephews or husbands or mothers, in order to encourage them to write the stories of their hearts.

For we all have stories. And they must be told. In telling our stories we affirm our selves, our very being, and thereby the purpose of our Creator and our lives.

To believe your own thought, to believe that what is true for you in your private heart is true for all men—that is genius.

RALPH WALDO EMERSON

FOR
WRITERS
ONLY

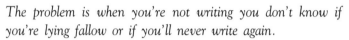

The problem is when you're not writing you don't know if you're lying fallow or if you'll never write again.

NORMAN MAILER

NERVES

Not long ago, a friend from California came to visit. He is a professional writer and the author of seven books. He had just finished his latest, a long and exhaustive memoir on which he had spent eight years and thousands of dollars in therapy. It was to be published the following year. We sat in the summer garden. He was sunk in apathy and despair.

"What is it about writing?" he asked, striking his forehead with the flat of his hand. "Why is it so awful? It's no way to live! Why do we do it?"

And then he leapt to his feet to walk unhappily around his chair. "Look at writers. I don't know a single writer who doesn't hate his work. Writers hate writing. They're always talking about how hard it is. Artists don't hate painting. You never hear an artist talking about how much he hates his work. Sculptors don't complain all the time about how hard they find sculpting. But writers . . . !"

A few weeks later I had occasion to ask an artist if she agreed. *Do* artists hate their work? She looked at me, amused.

"You're forgetting something," she said.

"What?"

"Writing is so powerful. People rarely look at a painting and weep."

True artists, whatever smiling faces they may show you, are obsessive, driven people . . .

JOHN GARDNER

No honest poet can ever feel quite sure of the permanence of what he has written; he may have wasted his time and messed up his life for nothing.

T. S. ELIOT

❈

My writer friend spent most of the weekend pouring out his depression and anxiety. He had forgotten that this is the way he always feels on the conclusion of a book (as many writers do). The phantoms of hell were panting at his neck.

It was not the writing that bothered him. It was the fact that he had nothing to write.

❈

"I'm sorry," he murmured. "I can't concentrate. What were you saying?" His ears buzzed. He was going through one of the worst panics of a writer's life, the I'll-never-be-a-writer stage. Here he was fifty-five years old, with seven books behind him, and none of them having made the *New York Times* bestseller list, though they were good books, entertaining, witty and literate, his whole soul poured into every one.

"I shouldn't have left TV, that's all. I was a fool. I had a job. I was being paid a salary to write. I enjoyed it. What did I do? I went off to write a book—a number of books—not thinking ahead. And now here I am, unemployable. Who wants to hire a man like me? All I've done is write. I'm not useful for anything. I'm too old."

❈

When you're not writing you have plenty of time for fear.

Correcting galleys helps. Reading proofs. But that work is not *real writing*. Friends come up and congratulate you on your finished book, and you look back at them, savagely. You give a sickly grin. "Thank you." You barely manage to muster the memory of manners, and you must

Life without work—I would commit suicide. Therefore work is more important than life.

K A T H E R I N E   M A N S F I E L D

There is no pleasure in the world like writing well and going fast. It's like nothing else. It's like a love affair, it goes on and on, and doesn't end in marriage. It's all courtship.

T E N N E S S E E   W I L L I A M S

forcibly remind yourself that they're right—yes, yes, it must be good to have finished your book. In fact you remember how, one day, it was. One day you put down your pen (or turned off the computer) and thought with a surge of undiluted joy—"I've done it! Finished!" And you were laughing to yourself because secretly you knew you still had weeks of playful work to do, editing, smoothing, polishing the sharp white stones. Or else you thought you'd use this freely flowing fine good energy to start another work.

Instead, in two days you collapse.

※

Now you enter another even more horrible period. Not only are you barren, but it drives you mad to think of better, more disciplined writers who never fell prey to weakness or to strain. Charles Dickens, Honoré de Balzac, Dumas père, Anthony Trollope writing their two thousand or three thousand words a day with manic precision.

※

Still, when most writers I know finish up a big project—a single book that took a year to write, two years, three—when they're coming into the home stretch and enjoying the high-flying gallop for the post, stretched out with the thunder of hooves in their ears, they think: "I can carry on like this forever. Once past the post, I'll start a second race."

If they are not in the midst of that next piece of work well before the first one ends, they are caught in the depression that my California friend expressed that day in the garden, unable to understand why the gift of words has been removed.

The writer is also a fool. He is the easiest man in the world to belittle, ridicule, dismiss, and scorn; and that also is precisely as it should be. He is also mad, measurably so, but saner than all the others with best sanity, the only sanity worth bothering about—the living, creative, vulnerable, valorous, unintimidated, and arrogant sanity of a free man.

WILLIAM SAROYAN

I would get up every morning, go to my office and write without qualms until I felt it was time to go home. As I neared the end I was too frightened that I might lose the conclusion— which I did not know yet—and so I merely sat in the garden and wrote in a notebook. I suddenly felt an enormous tension; but my ending, when it came, surprised me into laughter. I felt like a spectator at my own game.

ANITA BROOKNER

❈

"Why do you ask yourself if you're a writer?" said my sister one day when I'd been howling out my pain. "What an irrelevant question! As if it were some God-given grace, like saintliness or something!"

All right. Many writers, I suppose, are not "born writers." They work.

On the other hand, what my sister did not understand is the obsession to create. Writers need to write. That's why you panic at the completion of a play or novel. When you aren't writing you aren't certain you exist.

❈

Virginia Woolf suffered "acute nervous tension" whenever she neared the end of a novel. It's what my California friend was talking about—that terror of falling into the void of structureless free-fall freedom. One friend of mine has been working on her book for nearly fifteen years. She even went to a therapist to learn why finishing it felt like death.

The imagination is not subject to the will of the artist. To accept the fruits as gifts is to acknowledge that we are not their owners or masters, that we are, if anything, their servants, their ministers.

LEWIS HYDE

I felt very strongly that nothing depended on my will, that everything I might accomplish in life would not be won by my own efforts, but given as a gift.

CZESLAW MILOSZ

THE
GIFT

In the privacy of their most secret hearts, most writers, artists, actors, and musicians believe their talent is a gift. It comes from beyond the self, crashing over them unexpectedly—with joy. It is received, therefore, with awe and in humility.

Occasionally one will speak out unembarrassed by the thought of grace, except she knows that the blessing, this talent, must be treasured and nurtured, worked at, sought out . . . if only she knew how. And therefore it is not to be taken lightly, not cast before pig's feet or held aloft to the derision of people who don't understand. That is why many artists speak of it only amongst themselves, secretly, one on one, in quiet voices, fearful of losing it, grateful and awed.

☒

Who knows the driving force behind the art? Zora Neal Hurston wrote in her autobiography that she felt "commanded" to write her subject matter. Likewise, Harriet Beecher Stowe thought *Uncle Tom's Cabin* was written through her by Another Hand, so little did she know what

I was in the particular hell of the poet: a longish dry period. It was 1952, I was forty-four, and I thought I was done. I had been teaching the five-beat line for weeks—I knew quite a bit about it, but write it myself—no: So I felt myself a fraud.

Suddenly, in the early evening, the poem "The Dance" started, and finished itself in a very short time—say thirty minutes it was all done. I felt, I knew, I had hit it. I walked around and I wept; and I knelt down—I always do after I've written what I know is a good piece. But at the same time I had, as God is my witness, the actual sense of a Presence—as if Yeats himself were in that room. The house was charged with a psychic presence: the very walls seemed to shimmer. I wept for joy.

THEODORE ROETHKE

Isaiah (or was it Elisha?) was caught up into Heaven in a chariot of fire once. But when the weather is divine and I am free to work, such a journey is positively nothing.

KATHERINE MANSFIELD

was going to happen from moment to moment in the book. She was herself amazed at what she was writing.

She was thirty-nine when she began *Uncle Tom's Cabin*. She had given birth to seven children and seen one die. She wrote her book to be serialized in an abolitionist newspaper. Much of it she composed on the kitchen table in between the cooking, mending, tending to her house. . . .

※

Handel, like many artists, produced enormous works in a manic frenzy in short periods of time. He wrote *The Messiah* in something like twenty days.

On the third day of composing, he was fasting—too busy to stop to eat or drink—as the Hallelujah chorus, the angels singing at the birth of Christ, poured out of him. And then he began to hallucinate. . . .

"I did think I did see all Heaven before me, and the great God Himself."

※

But how do you court the Muse? How do you get Inspiration to approach? Without which you feel you lack identity.

Ninety percent of the work of writing is internal, and only ten percent happens at the typewriter.

ANONYMOUS

It's nervous work. The state you need to write in is the state that others are paying large sums to get rid of.

SHIRLEY HAZZARD

The author must keep his mouth shut when his work starts to speak.

FRIEDRICH NIETZSCHE

GETTING STARTED

Beginning is the hardest part. You roam the house, your rooms, the streets. You are jerked on the leash of your unease. Everything is calling to you—plants, children, animals, or worse, the need to make money: weed me, water me, feed me, pay me, clean me, tend me, buy me; while inside anxiety and tension curl like the edge of an oyster cooking.

⊗

This stage hurts. You hardly seem present on the physical plane. You neglect your duties. Your eyes turn inward. Your social life sours. You ache.

You have no choice. Your only alternative is to go to the limit of tolerable pain, to embrace it.

If you talk the story out, you lose the tension. You give away the need to write. Therefore, you can't even tell what you are thinking about to your wife or husband or lover or friend.

⊗

If you complain about it, you diminish the pain, but you

A story is like something you wind out of yourself. Like a spider, it is a web you weave, and you love your story like a child.

KATHERINE ANNE PORTER

In writing a novel, there is in the beginning what I would call a theme. It's not an idea but a feeling. Then this feeling goes on developing and unravelling itself, like a rope. This is why I say a novel writes itself. One writes a novel in order to know why one writes it. It is the same with life—you live not for some end, but in order to know why you live.

ALBERTO MORAVIA

also reduce the temperature of the story cooking deep inside.

With the force of a capped volcano the tension must build.

As yet, nothing is flowing onto paper. You feel sick.

You are hell to live with, irritable, your nerves on edge. The most you can do when someone approaches is to give a wild mad stare and flee. "I'm out of sorts," you mumble incoherently.

In your heart you know you are writing, and it is not going well.

⊗

A guest at a dinner party observed the strange expression on James Thurber's face.

"Don't be concerned," said Thurber's wife. "He's writing."

⊗

Experience has taught me that this pain is essential to the task. It defines two kinds of worrying: destructive and creative anxiety. The destructive kind brings you awake at night in panic and prevents your going back to sleep. The thoughts sweep like bats behind your eyes: Fear! Fear! Fear!

Destructive anxiety serves no useful purpose. It comes of its own accord, a state of fear, which afterwards finds something—anything—to attach itself to and be afraid about: money, love, work, war, death, the wasted lives of your children. Whatever you are afraid of is of less significance than the *fact* of anxiety. It is the fear that attacks: the content will pass to nothing when the assault recedes.

Those are the signs of destructive anxiety.

We have an interval and then our place knows us no more. Our one chance lies in expanding that interval, in getting as many pulsations as possible into the given time. Great passions may give us this quickened sense of life, ecstasy and sorrow of love, the various forms of enthusiastic activity, disinterested or otherwise, which come naturally to many of us. Only be sure it is passion—that it does yield you this fruit of a quickened, multiplied consciousness.

VICTOR HUGO

If we had to say what writing is, we would have to define it essentially as an act of courage.

CYNTHIA OZICK

I think I am a verb instead of a personal pronoun. A verb signifies to be, to do, to suffer. I signify all these.

ULYSSES S. GRANT

⊗

Creative anxiety, on the other hand, must be treasured. Like its destructive sister, it crucifies the writer. It carries with it real suffering and physical distress: migraines, backache, and especially, the anguish of an aching soul.

But it cannot be avoided if you are going to write. Its presence is part of the preparation, and must be welcomed, therefore, as a guest. The writer comforts himself that this incubation period varies from project to project, hours to days to weeks; and he draws on all the forces of his spirit to endure it, calls up courage, which is, as Rollo May puts it, "the capacity to move ahead in spite of despair." He calls on courage because nothing else is left.

⊗

One day I was sitting at my typewriter (Olympia electric: the second typewriter I'd ever owned, and still not self-correcting). I was paralyzed by fear. I sat with my elbows on the typewriter, my face in my hands, weak with pain. Trying to think my way out of it. Praying. Suddenly it occurred to me that the alternative to pain was not happiness—it was death. So long as I chose to be alive I would undergo anxiety. That was the price of living. I *chose* anxiety.

In that moment the anxiety vanished, and I began to write again.

⊗

I write on yellow-lined legal pads. I write diagonally against the lines, beginning with one short, curt word at the smallest triangle in the upper left-hand corner of the page. Underneath come two words, and under these fit

Beginning to write, you discover what you have to write about.

KIT REED

If an artist does not spring to his work as a soldier to the breach, if once within the crater he does not labor as a miner buried in the earth, if he contemplates his difficulties instead of conquering them one by one, the work remains unachieved, production becomes impossible, and the artist assists the suicide of his own talent.... The solution of the problem can be found only through incessant and sustained work. . . . True artists, true poets, generate and give birth today, tomorrow, ever. From this habit of labor results a ceaseless comprehension of difficulties which keep them in communion with the muse and her creative forces.

HONORÉ DE BALZAC

When I work I relax; doing nothing or entertaining visitors makes me tired.

PICASSO

three, and so the lines flow out onto the legal pad growing in two columns of cramped small script, or else in two great awkward isosceles triangles. Each triangle will take up a fully typed eight-by-ten page, so small are these letters. They are the legs of insects, defiantly crossing the straight blue rigid legal lines. My first draft is formless, creative, unconfined by someone else's rules of how a line should look or where on the page the letters must be spaced.

⊗

This is the period of BEGINNING.

I lie on my back on my bed, whittling at a legal pad.

I sit at the typewriter staring out the window at the soft, sweet, misty rain, the water tenderly rippling down toward the gutter, the tree trunks black with rain, and where are the birds, I wonder. Where do they go in the silent rain? Wouldn't you think you would see them shivering on a branch? For that matter, where do they go when they die? We hear of the elephant graveyards, where the elephants go to die, but how much more curious it is that birds are not falling out of the sky all the time, on our heads, at our feet, dying and falling and flopping to the ground. I rarely see a dead bird on the ground.

I sit at the typewriter—or lie on my bed—making foolish notes on paper that will never see the light of publication, but which help free up my hand, my mind. It doesn't matter what you write at this stage—only that you keep in practice. Every day.

⊗

"But how do you begin?" a friend cried out to me yesterday. "I don't know how to begin!"

The thing about writers that people don't realize is that a lot of what they do is play. You know, playing around with. That doesn't mean that it isn't serious or that it doesn't have a serious meaning or a serious intention.

MARGARET ATWOOD

I never had much patience with women who said, "Well, I can't work this week or next week or the week after, but maybe I'll work in six months' time or maybe in a years' time." I found one had to do some work every day, even at midnight, because either you're a professional or not.

BARBARA HEPWORTH

My advice is sometimes contradictory, parsed out according to the person's need. To her, I said, "It's simple. You choose a place that is yours to write. All you do in that single spot is write—no bills, no phone calls, no reading in that space: it is reserved for writing. Then you go there every morning, and you sit at your desk, whether you have anything to say or not. You stare at the blank paper, and you fiddle with your pen, and you draw pictures if you have to, and you sit there for the two hours that you have allotted as your writing time, or three, or four. You do not move. Your back hurts. Your butt, your brain; and still you sit and look at that pad of paper (or word processor, if you wish). If you write nothing the first day, you go back the next, and if you write nothing, you return once more, and still you sit for the allotted time. . . . By the third day, out of sheer boredom, you will write."

I think it is like a spiritual discipline. You go to the zazen and bow 108 times to the ground, and you hate it, and still you go every day and do your sitting and walking meditations and bow 108 times a day. And why? Because you trust yourself; you know you'll receive the reward.

⊗

Best to read nothing now. Best to let the boredom build.

Best to avoid much time with people, talking, reacting, responding. Social intercourse takes energy, dilutes the pain, but also the creative anxiety.

⊗

"How do you write?" she asked another time.

It's simple. You get up in the morning and say to yourself, "Oh, goody! I get to see what happens to Julie today!" (or to Frank or Elwin, or whatever is your hero's name).

Of the legion of women who toy with arts and letters, very few persevere; and even those who pass this first obstacle will very often continue to be torn between their narcissism and an inferiority complex. Inability to forget themselves is a defect that will weigh more heavily upon them than upon women in any other career; if their essential aim is the formal satisfaction of success, they will not give themselves over to the contemplation of the world; they will be incapable of re-creating it in art.

SIMONE DE BEAUVOIR

In art, the self becomes self-forgetful.

FLANNERY O'CONNOR

Anything alive that makes demands, arouses in me an infinite capacity to give it its due, the consequences of which completely use me up.

RAINER MARIA RILKE

It is work. But "easy" or "difficult" are only judgments created by our thought, and when we go very deep and still, such distinctions no longer apply. It is the going deep that's hard.

I think that creativity is about reaching to the soul, connecting to the inner Self so totally that no difference exists between inner and outer, good and bad, reality and fiction, past and future. Everything rests in the utter and magnificent I AM.

I remember once working at my typewriter, deep in thought, when I glanced up at the tree outside my window, and for a startling moment I *was* the tree—no separation—and also the air between the tree and me, the glass of the windowpane, the story I was writing, paper, typewriter, and myself.

Satori, I thought, and with the naming, which constitutes a movement back into conscious Mind, I wrenched out of that sweet state, and I was looking at the page again, marveling at what had happened, and how to reach that suspension of time and Self again. . . .

⊗

Rainer Maria Rilke left his wife and baby, so much did he need to listen for his inner voice, his Muse. Years later the poet would not even attend his daughter's wedding, and when the newlyweds asked to come visit for a few hours during their honeymoon, he refused. He had no boundaries, apparently, as if he were so open that he became the world around him. He had no way to guard his inner voice.

But other writers thrive on busy-ness. I think of Bertolt Brecht writing in the midst of his noisy friends—or of the poet Frank O'Hara, notorious for binging while

If a story is in you, it has got to come out.

WILLIAM FAULKNER

Only a mediocre writer is always at his best.

W. SOMERSET MAUGHAM

You must write, not just think you're going to. . . . And you must widen your vocabulary, enjoy words. You must read widely, not in order to copy, but to find your own voice. It's a matter of going through life with all one's senses alive, to be responsive to experience, to other people.

P. D. JAMES

writing—or of J. S. Bach, the father of many children, composing his immortal fugues and melodies while the head of a happy household. Or one woman friend of mine who writes stories, films, articles, novels, all the while caring for five dogs and I don't know how many horses on her New Mexico ranch, and teaching writing and also acting as a wife and as the mother to a teenage girl. You just do it.

⚮

Every day you are afraid. Every day you move through fear to your desk, and as soon as you pick up your pen, or read the sentence left over from the night before, incomplete, needing an adjustment in rhythm—a stronger verb, a slash of color or the taste of bitter herbs—in that moment of solving the problems all fear dissolves. You are writing again.

Rest is not idleness, and to lie sometimes on the grass under the trees on a summer's day, listening to the murmur of water, or watching the clouds float across the sky, is by no means a waste of time.

SIR JOHN LUBBOCK

I have a basic indolence about me which is essential to writing. . . . It's thinking time, it's hanging-out time, it's daydreaming time. You know, it's lie-around-the-bed time, it's sitting-like-a-dope-in-your-chair time. And that seems to me essential to any work.

GRACE PALEY

It takes a heap of loafing to write a book.

GERTRUDE STEIN

WALKING-
AROUND
TIME

Many instructors of playwrighting or fiction advise their
students from the earliest planning stages to make an outline or "write it down." This is not necessarily sound. Too
early an attempt to snatch at rainbows results in their van-
ishing entirely. We do better to memorize the colors, inte-
grate the memory, and later try to re-create what it was we
saw.

☒

I know one writer who begins new work by playing the piano. When writing she has no time for music, and when
depressed or disgruntled or anxious about her work with
words she does not care to play. But at some point she will
notice, like the first delicate tendrils of unfolding spring,
an urge to play the piano. For hours she sits, practicing the
same Czerny exercises, the few Clementi sonatas that she
knows. She is lost in the music, and when she wakes up
from the fit, she is always pleased; for she knows it signi-

Wasting time. The old cry—the first and last cry—why do ye tarry? Ah, why indeed? My deepest desire is to be a writer, to have "a body of work" done. And there the work is, there the stories wait for me, grow tired, wilt, fade because I will not come. And I hear and acknowledge them, and still I go on sitting at the window, playing with the ball of wool.

KATHERINE MANSFIELD

As for my next book I am going to hold myself from writing it till I have it impending in me: grown heavy in my mind like a ripe pear; pendent, gravid, asking to be cut or it will fall.

VIRGINIA WOOLF

Inspirations never go in for long engagements; they demand immediate marriage to action.

BRENDAN FRANCIS

fies a work is being born. She does not know what form the story will take yet, or what plot. But with the anticipation of a mountain climber she knows that soon she will be in high altitudes, walking on the cold white glacier again.

One day the words begin.

⚔

For another writer I know, the story comes like a whisper in a crowd—a chiffon scarf ghosting past; and it must be caught the quicker for that.

⚔

And then there is my friend, a writer-editor-sculptor-poet, in Maine. He writes the stories in his head, long, wonderful tales of his friend Albert, which he is certain he will soon get down on paper, when he gets a chance. He will be walking on the seashore, writing in his imagination; or driving in the car; and the stories come and he is laughing to himself, or feeling the pinch of sorrow, and loving the stories, listening. . . .

Later, when he goes to write them down, he's lost the voice. He knew the stories so well. He thought all he needed was the leisure to write them down. . . . But it's not true. . . . Your feeling goes away. The story dies on you.

That's where the discipline and sheer grit and lust to win come through.

There's a time, therefore, when it's important to move right on to ink.

⚔

When it is going well, the words flow off your fingertips; you are immersed in the music. You could not possibly tell

The pages are still blank, but there is a miraculous feeling of the words all being there, written in invisible ink and clamoring to become visible. You might, if you chose, develop any part of the picture, for the idea of sequence does not really exist as far as the author is concerned. Sequence arises only because words have to be written one after the other on consecutive pages, just as the reader's mind must have time to go through the book, at least the first time he reads it. If the mind were constructed on optional lines and if a book could be read in the same way as a painting is taken in by the eye, that is, without the bother of working from left to right, and without the absurdity of beginnings and ends, this would be the ideal way of appreciating a novel, for thus the author saw it at the moment of conception.

VLADIMIR NABOKOV

The first four months of writing the book, my mental image is scratching with my hands through granite. My other image is pushing a train up the mountain, and it's icy, and I'm in bare feet.

MARY HIGGINS CLARK

anyone what songs you are hearing, what ecstasies you feel.

"I listen to the voices," said Faulkner.

⊗

You begin by hard work and discipline, digging in the dirt until your fingers are bloody; and suddenly the characters find themselves. The setting is in place. The cellos have picked up the mood and are keeping the whole together, while in the background a low drum beats. Now you have only to watch the characters and write down what they say.

At such moments you are in what August Wilson calls the "land of magic." And, with the words flowing forth, nothing, nothing in the world, can equal the pleasure— not skiing or sailing, not sex, not flying off cliffs with wings strapped to your shoulders—because in those pure moments you are in perfect balance, soaring with the uni-verse.

⊗

The bubble bursts.

It does always.

The next moment you are lying bloody at the foot of the cliff. Common sense comes rushing in, drags you from your trance and leaves you sitting stunned and sheepish with your work. You go away. The next day you find that what you wrote needs editing, or else you find that subse-quent words crawl as painfully as worms out of your living flesh.

I remember once asking him if he wanted to write. He laughed and said he had nothing to write about. "That's the most inconclusive reason for not writing that I've ever heard," I smiled.

W. SOMERSET MAUGHAM

I could not live by literature if only, to begin with, because of the slow maturing of my work and its special character.

FRANZ KAFKA

ON KNOWING
YOU ARE A
WRITER

Last night I was asked again, "When did you first know you were a writer? Did you always know?" In the backs of their minds just nudging at their consciousness you see the next question floating, perhaps still formless, embryonic: "And what of me? Can I be a real writer too?"

I want to cry out, Yes! Just *start*. Sure, Gore Vidal published his first novel at the age of twenty-one. And P. D. James, the mystery writer, was in her thirties. But George Bernard Shaw did not write a play until he was forty-two, and Norman Maclean did not publish *A River Runs Through It*—and he only wrote two books—until he was in his seventies. Anita Brookner began fiction-writing in middle age. Looking at my own work, I take heart that George Eliot, Joseph Conrad, Edith Wharton, Isak Dinesen, and Joyce Cary were all in their forties or close to it before they began (and Conrad, Polish, had never written in English before); that Laura Ingalls Wilder was in her sixties when she wrote *Little House on the Prairie* . . . that

Artists are the antennae of the race.

EZRA POUND

It must be five times as hard to become a proficient writer as to become a proficient doctor, mainly because there is no true and tried education process for a writer, so every fellow who wants to write for profit, including my daughter Nora, must be prepared for a long, slow, and often very discouraging preparation. But if he's got it in him to be a writer, this won't stop him. If he stops, it's a fair sign that he was never intended to be a writer in the first place.

NUNNALLY JOHNSON

Writing is not apart from living. Writing is a kind of double living. The writer experiences everything twice: once in reality and once more in the mirror which waits always before and behind him.

DONALD MURRAY

Sophocles wrote *Oedipus at Colonnus*, one of the master-pieces of literature and theater, when in his eighties. . . . There's time, I tell myself . . . if I hurry . . . if I don't waste time now. . . .

⊗

I first knew I was a writer at the age of ten, when I failed my fifth-grade English exam. The reason I failed was be-cause the first problem was "Finish this paragraph," and two blue books and forty-five minutes later, when the bell rang, I was still writing. I had not finished the paragraph and came out of the writer's trance abashed and confused. I never got to question two.

No one laughed. My parents and teachers said, "Oh, she's a writer." As if that explained something. But I felt ashamed.

It took another fifteen years before I dared, tenta-tively, to try to learn. I didn't know Frank O'Connor's ad-age: "Work chooses the Man."

My childhood was devoid of writers. I had no role models. It did not occur to me to sit at the kitchen table every night like the Brontë children (Charlotte, Emily, Anne, Branwell), scribbling my novels into infinitesimal small secret notebooks, or reading them out loud to my sister or brother (good heavens!). It did not occur to me to write: I was busy riding horses and struggling with school (hard enough without adding *writing*!) and coping with living, having adventures, reading. . . . I had no time to write.

The aim of every artist is to arrest motion, which is life, by artificial means and hold it fixed. . . .

WILLIAM FAULKNER

It is difficult
to get the news from poems
yet men die miserable every day
for lack
of what is found there.

WILLIAM CARLOS WILLIAMS

You must once and for all give up being worried about successes and failures. Don't let that concern you. It's your duty to go on working steadily day by day, quite steadily, to be prepared for mistakes, which are inevitable, and for failures.

ANTON CHEKHOV

⊗

Another image from childhood comes to mind. It is myself as a young girl, curled in my father's overstuffed armchair in the study, reading the *Iliad*. I had come to the description of a hero's death, where Homer says no finer end can anyone have than on the battlefield; and the hero's deeds shall ring down the corridors of time, made immortal in men's memory. I remember thinking, "No! That's not what I want! I want to be the one who *writes* about the hero's death!"

It was thrilling to hold that book in my hand and realize that three thousand years earlier the author had transcribed a scene into a sequence of tiny black squiggles on a page, this intricate embroidery of curving strokes, which I, a child, lying in my father's chair three (imagine!) or four millennia later, could by some magic of the inner mind translate back into the very visions he had seen, images and emotions so powerful they brought tears to my eyes. From little black figures on a page.

There, I thought, lies immortality.

⊗

Of course, you write nothing, faced with such an ideal. You cannot think of audience when working. If you allowed yourself to think, as you were writing, that anyone would read your words—would judge and criticize and view your inner heart—your brain would go blank in self-defense. You could not move.

And this is not an idle thought. It is a spiritual principle, a law, like Heisenberg's Principle of Indeterminacy—in which the scientist discovered that the light turned on in order to observe the atomic particles changed the objects viewed. . . .

I think, to a poet, the human community is like the community of birds to a bird, singing to each other. Love is one of the reasons we are singing to one another, love of language itself, love of sound, love of singing itself, and love of the other birds.

SHARON OLDS

And still your unnamed longings eat at you. It would take another forty years before I found the spiritual director who one day murmured to me gently, "Did you ever consider that God puts longings in our hearts in order that we execute them?"

How do I know what I think until I see what I say?

One of the most difficult things is the first paragraph. I have spent many months on a first paragraph, and once I get it, the rest just comes out very easily.

GABRIEL GARCÍA MÁRQUEZ

WAITING
SPINNING
DRIFTING

It is the act of writing that produces ideas, not the other way around. Rudyard Kipling referred to this phenomenon when he said he had to "drift, wait and obey" the *daemon* in him.

Therefore you write every day, whether you have anything to say or not, and you must be prepared to throw it all away. Not everything is worth keeping.

Reading through the previous day's writing sometimes helps to start.

If you leave a sentence incomplete or a thought half finished, you can pick up the next morning's work more quickly.

※

Thornton Wilder took long walks before beginning work. Willa Cather read a page of the Bible every day. I know writers who do not disdain to pray, and I shall say more about this later, but for the moment, consider the prayer

My feeling is if you need a reward to tempt yourself to reach
a personal goal, the goal may not be worth reaching. What you
do instead of your real work is your real work.

ROGER EBERT

Only a mediocre writer is always at his best.

W. SOMERSET MAUGHAM

I don't wait for moods. You accomplish nothing if you do that.
Your mind must know it has got to get down to work.

PEARL BUCK

of Katherine Mansfield: "May I be worthy to do it! Lord, make me crystal clear for thy light to shine through."

❈

Writing is so hard. My god, this first-draft writing is so hard that sometimes in the beginning, before the work itself takes over, carrying you on its flood, you must give yourself rewards.

"When I write this chapter I can call my boyfriend."

"When I finish one page more I can get an ice cream cone."

"If I write this section, I'll find a check in the mail."

❈

And sometimes the work is so boring you think you'll scream. For one book, I made up a game. I would look through the dictionary until I found an obscure and magnificent word, then use it in the text. I remember once constructing an entire chapter of the book I was working on around one word (*autochthons*), and the puzzle was to do it in such a way that no one knew the word came first. That was when I was writing nonfiction, before I took the novel's dare.

❈

You wake up at seven or eight in the morning, and wander around, puttering, "fiddling around," drinking coffee, or cleaning up the kitchen, or taking a walk with the dogs, or looking at the dew on the garden grass. Finally there is no excuse. You go to your desk.

❈

To some people, planning is more fun than writing. Fred-

The best part about writing is stopping.

COLIN WALTERS

You do not even have to leave your room. Remain sitting at your table and listen. Do not even listen, simply wait. Do not even wait, be still and solitary. The world will freely offer itself to you to be unmasked, it has no choice, it will roll in ecstasy at your feet.

FRANZ KAFKA

erick Forsyth, author of *The Day of the Jackal* and other books, claims to hate writing and to do it only because he loves research, and William Gaddis is reported to have "twenty pages of research behind every paragraph" of *The Recognitions*, his 1955 novel about fakes and counterfeiting. In fact, when you have not been writing for weeks, when "the pipes are clogged," to use the image of Larry McMurtry, so that the writing cannot flow, then anything is more fun than writing. Erasing is more fun, changing a typewriter ribbon, getting more coffee, sharpening pencils, painting a room, answering the telephone. Any interruption brings relief from the discipline of trying to use words well. Anne Beattie used to vacuum rather than write.

⊗

When I am happiest, I write almost every day. For long periods, however, my time is taken. Days pass . . . weeks. Then I forget all over again how to write. I forget I can begin. I forget I ever once began. At times like these, then, fear and doubt must be fought with all the weapons in our arsenal. These include: affirmations, prayer, silence, stillness, trusting, trying, waiting, walking, reading, not reading. Writing about my fear, and writing this book now to remind myself of how creation comes.

⊗

This is the time of listening. You are trying to hear the inner siren's song at the center of your soul. You take little stabs at writing. You hold the pen and write a phrase. And pause, for the Voice is gone. Too frail. Too weak. You draw pictures to give presence to the pen.

⊗

Just as appetite comes by eating, so work brings inspiration, if inspiration is not discernible at the beginning.

IGOR STRAVINSKY

The main thing I try to do is write as clearly as I can. Because I have the greatest respect for the reader, and if he's going to the trouble of reading what I've written—I'm a slow reader myself and I guess most people are—why, the least I can do is make it as easy as possible for him to find out what I'm trying to say, trying to get at. I rewrite a good deal to make it clear.

E. B. WHITE

Good writers are those who keep the language efficient. That is to say, keep it accurate, keep it clear.

EZRA POUND

"Get black on white," said Guy de Maupassant, knowing that the task of the first draft is to get words down regardless of quality.

※

Frank O'Connor, the Irish short story writer and novelist, likewise withheld all initial critical judgment. "I don't care what the writing's like [at this stage]," he said. "Any sort of rubbish. It's the design of the story which is the most important."

※

Some things will drive anyone to write. These include:
- housework
- looking at the dust on the apartment floor
- the company of boring people
- cleaning a septic tank
- considering one's death
- worrying about the children's school bills
- hearing a good story

※

It was Émile Zola who kept a motto in his workroom: *Nulla dies sine linea.* "No day without lines." He wrote one thousand to fifteen hundred words a day, until in thirty-one years he finished with businesslike dispatch something like twenty-five novels and twenty-three other books. When you have nothing to say, you write anyway, if only to keep in practice.

I see but one rule: to be clear.

STENDHAL

Daydreaming had started me on the way; but story writing once I was truly in its grip, took me and shook me awake.

EUDORA WELTY

⁂

One day when I was particularly bad-tempered my child made a sign for me and put it over my desk: *Avez-vous ecrit aujourd'hui?* "Have you written today?"

An essential portion of any artist's labor is not creation so much as invocation.

LEWIS HYDE

O for a muse of fire, that would ascend the brightest heaven of invention!

WILLIAM SHAKESPEARE

PRAYER
AND
INVOCATION

In ancient times when a singer stood before the banquet table, lyre in his hand, and struck the chord that hushed the assembled guests, what were his first words?

"O Muse, fill my mouth with your songs. Make me silver-tongued that my words may pierce the hearts of men. . . ."

Later, college English teachers would tell you that this was no more than a literary tradition, the requisite invocation to the Muse.

But writers know it's real. At some point, consciously or not, we invoke our gods, the *daemon* of the Greeks, the *genius* of the Romans, the genie, the Muse, the spirits of past Masters calling to us, called back by their love of words. We invoke the Lady in white, our angels, our guides, asking for the highest levels of creative power.

⊗

The artist rachets back and forth between grandiosity and

Modesty is a virtue not often found among poets, for almost every one of them thinks himself the greatest in the world.

MIGUEL DE CERVANTES

The men like to put me down as the best woman painter. I think I'm one of the best painters.

GEORGIA O'KEEFE

the inadequacy that comes of collapsing ego. Knowing this, the artist props up the constant failure of heart. Enrico Caruso, the great tenor, used to pace in the wings before an opera, warming up with the other singers. While the others practiced scales and phrases they soon would sing on stage, Caruso would belt out, full-voice: "I AM THE GREATEST SINGER OF ALL TIME! I AM THE GREATEST SINGER IN THE WORLD!"

It reminds me of the advice my father used to give to my sister and me as we were preparing to go out on a date.

"Turn. Let me see you," he would say approvingly. "You look beautiful." Then he would add the words he always said before we went out—words that every daughter needs a father to say: "Now remember, before you go in to the dance, pause a moment at the doorway, lift your head, and tell yourself, 'I am the most beautiful girl at the ball.' And only *then* go in."

He was teaching us confidence. "Remember to compliment the boy you're dancing with. If you can't think of anything else to say, compliment his tie. You have no idea how scared boys are." And concerning our shyness at "working" a large party: "Stop thinking about yourself. Everyone there is more afraid than you. It's your responsibility to put someone else at ease."

The same advice applies to the writer. Where do you put your attention? On fear or love? I wish the choice were made just once and not repeated every moment of the day.

※

I am a real writer! You whistle in the dark. *I have the conditions to create the work that is in me. I have talent, discipline, dedication, discernment. . . .*

Nothing is accomplished without enthusiasm.

RALPH WALDO EMERSON

❈

In the end, the gods help those also who help themselves.

There are so many different kinds of writing and so many ways to work that the only rule is this: do what works. Almost everything has been tried and found to succeed for somebody. The methods, even the ideas, of successful writers contradict each other in a most heartening way, and the only element I find common to all successful writers is persistence—an overwhelming determination to succeed. . . . They will *not* be thrust aside!

Writers kid themselves—about themselves and other people. Take the talk about writing methods. Writing is just work—there's no secret. If you dictate or use a pen or type or type with your toes—it is just work.

SINCLAIR LEWIS

HOW
(WITH WHAT
TOOLS)

If you don't have paper, any surface will do. Write on the backs of envelopes, or bills, or grocery lists, on paper bags. One playwright I know wrote much of the last act of a play in the margins of Barbara Tuchman's *Stillwell in China* when she had no paper with her in a car.

Paper beside your bed will capture a dream, a phrase, a word you've searched for all day long. At night you can be surprised by words.

⊗

Sometimes we make up stratagems to trick the Muse—or fool ourselves that we are not writing when we are. We find safe space: John Nichols, author of *The Milagro Beanfield War*, writes a lot in the tub at 4:00 A.M. "It's the only place not inundated with manuscripts, letters waiting to be answered." He writes by hand on the back of junk mail, then transfers his words to type on an old Olympia portable typewriter, bought for a hundred dollars in 1975.

When I sit down to write I feel extraordinarily at ease, and I move in an element which, it seems to me, I know extraordinarily well; I use tools that are familiar to me and they fit snugly in my hands.

NATALIA GINZBURG

The beauty of word processing, God bless my word processor, is that it keeps the plotting very fluid. The prose becomes like a liquid that you can manipulate at will. In the old days, when I typed, every piece of typing paper was like cast in concrete.

SUE GRAFTON

Remarks are not literature.

GERTRUDE STEIN

⊗

Tennessee Williams wrote *Cat on a Hot Tin Roof* on an assortment of hotel stationery. Then he sent off his only copy to his agent, by ordinary mail.

⊗

I used to favor colored paper—blue for the first draft, canary for the next, and pink for the third, perhaps, but never the terrifying purity of blank white bond until the book was nearly finished—almost set. The horror of a word processor came for me first in seeing my drafts printed on white paper, ameliorated only by the shadings of the screen, tints that diffuse the impression of a stark white page.

⊗

Jack Kerouac wrote *On the Road* all single-spaced on one long roll of paper, with no periods, commas, or paragraphs—thus inspiring Truman Capote's famous remark: "That's not writing, that's typing."

⊗

People ask writers all the time whether they write by hand or on a keyboard, be it word processor or typewriter. For me, the answer is both. When I'm having trouble I write by hand. There is some connection between the mind and the fingers that draws out words. Sometimes it is sufficient merely to take a pen and begin to scratch short stabbing M's in the upper left-hand corner of the sheet, small slanting strokes which turn in a few moments into a sawtooth frieze, iamboids joined in long lines; and suddenly they are forming letters and words and I'm off . . . writing faster and faster, filling pages furiously.

I see [my pen] as an extension of my musculature. It's like being a painter. It's the closest I can get to my breath.

SPALDING GRAY

It's a messy business. You wind up with shoe boxes of scrap paper.

CORMAC MCCARTHY

Talent is a question of quantity. Talent does not write one page: it writes three hundred.

JULES REYNARD

Natalie Goldberg, author of *Writing Down the Bones*, writes that any pen suffices, so long as it moves smoothly without catching on the paper. I add another caveat: the ink must last. Not long ago I discovered a new fine-point, black-ink, sweetly rolling ballpoint pen and bought a handful and used them happily until eight or ten months later when, hunting through my notes, I found the ink had faded. I could hardly read the words. Another year and nothing would remain: the crypto-dream of every spy.

Rudyard Kipling wrote superstitiously with the blackest possible ink on special blue paper.

Ernest Hemingway wrote in pencil on onionskin.

Athol Fugard, the South African playwright, chooses a new pen for each play, grinds his own ink, and retires each pen after the play is done.

⌘

Vladimir Nabokov wrote on lined Bristol index cards, shuffling them and writing scenes wherever he felt like it, regardless of the chronology. Later his wife typed out his manuscripts.

This is reminiscent of Robert Pirsig, author of *Zen and the Art of Motorcycle Maintenance*, who wrote his book on index cards. He had a shoebox full of index cards that he shuffled about into various orders, to his satisfaction. I am reminded of the Dadaist who pulled unrelated phrases from a hat to make his poetry—or William Burroughs, who combined the fragments of his mad poetry by haphazard use of scissors.

Count Leo Tolstoy also used scissors and paste. Each morning he attacked the writing of the previous day, cutting and rearranging the descriptions and scenes of *War and Peace* or *Anna Karenina*; by afternoon his worktable

Writing a book was an adventure. To begin with, it was a toy, an amusement; then it became a mistress, then a master, and then a tyrant.

WINSTON CHURCHILL

Like every writer's professional life, mine is spent doing a kind of dreaming—from the time I sit down at the desk and pick up my faithful fountain pen until the time I put the stuff on the Macintosh—which is a kind of waking up.

JOHN BARTH

Writing is easy. All you do is sit staring at the blank sheet of paper until the drops of blood form on your forehead.

RED SMITH

was covered with scraps of paper in orderly piles, which his wife dutifully recopied each night, after she had taken care of her house and accounts and the thirteen children. It is said that she recopied each page of *War and Peace* at least five times.

⊗

Today this cut-and-paste method is often handled by a friendly PC. But sometimes you still get down to basics—paper, scissors, staples, glue.

⊗

It took several years for me to shift to a word processor. Now I look back in amazement that I wrote four books on my then-husband's college typewriter—an Olympia manual portable, easily twenty years old. I typed and retyped, cutting and pasting, page after dreary page!

Often when using my laptop I have wondered: Do I read the text as carefully as if I had to retype every word again and again? Are the sentences less polished on a computer than composed by hand? Do we lose by processing, as it's called, the beautiful rhythms of our speech? Or do I simply forget, because it's not on pages before me, that now I'm working on draft 126?

Always, when in trouble, blocked by the difficulty of expression, I revert to pen and pad. It pleases me that Toni Morrison writes on yellow legal pads with "a nice number two pencil." John Barth uses his "faithful fountain pen," before he types into a Macintosh. John Updike uses pen or pencil, then the typewriter; and finally his secretary puts it all into a word processor.

⊗

My task—which I am trying to achieve—is by the power of the written word to make you hear, to make you feel. It is, before all, to make you see.

JOSEPH CONRAD

I do not write and never have written to an arranged plot. The book is composed at once, like a picture, and may start anywhere, in the middle or at the end. I may go from the end to the beginning in the same day, and then from the beginning to the middle.

JOYCE CARY

Annie Dillard tells how one day a seven-year-old boy told her how much he liked a particular story of hers. "Did you write it?" he asked, to her pleasure and surprise, and just as she was about to answer, added, "Or did you type it?"

⊗

I am told that some people dictate into a tape recorder. I can't imagine how: for me the sound of a voice tears apart the silent music of the page, the inner rhythms that resonate only to the human heart. I have heard other writers speak of this phenomenon, the need for silence, though after the words are down you can read them aloud, pacing your room and revising, and then the sound of your own voice does not get in the way.

⊗

I know a woman who shifts from word processor to pen to typewriter, so she'll never grow dependent on one tool. She's afraid that one day she'll find herself without her favorite pen and be unable to write. Her objective is to write anywhere, under any circumstance. In the sand if necessary.

⊗

Joyce Cary, author of sixteen books including *The Horse's Mouth*, wrote very fast, producing (like many writers) three times the material he finally used—writing in a frenzy of abundance, leaving passages incomplete and hurrying to further scenes—a kind of mental index card, for in his mind he knew where every scene would go. Later he would fill in and cut out, during the long slow lovely days of currying and grooming that a book demands.

At the end of his life, Cary, ill and handicapped,

If I had not been so great an invalid, I should not have done so much as I have accomplished.

CHARLES DARWIN

I have never believed that my limitations were in any sense punishments or accidents. If I had held such a view, I could never have expected the strength to overcome them.

HELEN KELLER

"Fool," said my muse to me, "Look in thy heart and write."

SIR PHILIP SIDNEY

wrote with his pen strapped to his hand, his arm in a brace. He worked on a single long scroll of paper threaded through an electrically operated writing machine that he had invented. And *still*, he wrote!

⊗

How you write is of less significance than the fact that it is done. Ved Mehta, the brilliant *New Yorker* writer, is blind, as were Homer, John Milton, and Jorge Luis Borges. James Joyce was nearly blind as he wrote *Ulysses*.

John Milton, when the voices would come upon him, would awaken his daughter in the middle of the night, to dictate his magnificent passages to her. She became a slave to his obsessions and his Muse.

Helen Keller, deaf and blind from the age of two, graduated from Radcliffe with honors, taught herself Latin, French, and some Greek, and wrote fourteen books.

Stephen W. Hawking, locked helpless in a wheelchair, unable to write by hand or even to speak clearly, has found with his computer the freedom to leap in his imagination into the very secrets of the universe and write them out for us.

Can I really complain that I have no time or talent to pursue my work?

All I needed was a steady table and typewriter. A marble topped bedroom washstand table made a good place; the dining room table between meals was also suitable.

AGATHA CHRISTIE

I am a completely horizontal author. I can't think unless I'm lying down, either in bed or stretched on a couch and with a cigarette and coffee handy.

TRUMAN CAPOTE

WHERE
(WHAT
SPACE)

Agatha Christie plotted her books anywhere—in the bathtub, as she tells us, eating apples. She found the warmth of the water conducive to the creative flow, and when you've withstood the English cold you appreciate her wisdom—as well as that of Barbara Cartland, dictating her books to rotating rounds of secretaries, who departed to type the pages up, as she luxuriated under a white quilt on a white sofa with her two white lapdogs.

⊗

Ernest Hemingway got up at first light, and from 5:00 A.M. to 10:00 A.M., he wrote standing up, shifting his weight from foot to foot. Only when the writing was flowing well did he move to a typewriter and a chair.

⊗

To some writers where they work can be as important as the other methods by which they entice the Muse. We

Writing is just a man alone in the room with the English language trying to make it come out right. The important thing is that your work be something no one else could do.

JOHN BERRYMAN

I have everything I need. A square of sky, a piece of stone, a page, a pen, and memory raining down on me in sleeves.

HARRIET DOERR

Usually I try to be there by six. Everything has been taken off the walls so that there's nothing to arrest my sight. On the bed I have Roget's Thesaurus, *a dictionary, a Bible, and a deck of playing cards.*

TONI MORRISON

think of Marcel Proust in his cork-lined bedroom, remembering the past. Or Truman Capote, who could write anywhere, he said, except in a room with yellow roses; or Honoré de Balzac, hiding from his creditors and consuming gallons of coffee as he poured out volumes of *The Human Comedy*; or Jane Austen, working in the parlor of the house in Chaston, at a little round table hardly large enough to hold her notebook. She was so shy that at the squeak of the door, she hurriedly put away her work. The squeaking hinge protected her privacy, and out of respect for her the household kept the hinge unoiled.

Virginia Woolf wanted a room of her own and Mary McCarthy simply "a nice peaceful place with some good light."

But most writers make do with whatever is on hand, and I know one woman who quarreled furiously with her husband when he insisted on disturbing her work space by painting the ugly plaster walls of "her" room, so little did she care about the surroundings where she worked. "I'm not looking at the walls!" she cried, impatient at being interrupted even for a time.

It can be big or small—a corner of the bedroom, a garret, an attic furnished with desk and lamp and chair. . . . One writer wants a small and cozy space. Another needs space, believing that the larger the room and the more panoramic the view, the bigger and more ambitious are the thoughts that germinate in it.

Toni Morrison, though she has a large house in North Carolina, keeps a hotel room for work. She gets up at 5:00 A.M., makes coffee and takes it to the hotel. Then she watches the light come up—the ritual being important—and with the light, she begins. Jane Smiley has worked in restaurants, with babies on her lap.

I must have a room to myself, which shall be my room. I have in my own mind pitched on Mrs. Whipple's room. We can put the stove in it. I have bought a carpet. . . .

HARRIET BEECHER STOWE

All my major works have been written in prison. . . . I would recommend prison not only to aspiring writers but to aspiring politicians, too.

JAWAHARLAL NEHRU

I know one writer who cannot compose new material if anyone is in the room with her, even if the other person is only reading quietly. She feels the alien vibrations. They grate on her nerves: she cannot hear her inner voices, so noisy is the throbbing in the room. But she can edit and rewrite anywhere—on a subway, in a museum, at the noisy base camp of a ski resort. . . . Natalie Goldberg, on the other hand, urges her students to move to an unfamiliar place if they hit a snag—a café—a park bench—any place different from where they usually compose.

⊗

Prison can also provide a productive place to work, as Cervantes and John Bunyan can testify. Oscar Wilde, on the other hand, was not given pen and paper until the last nine months of his two-year prison stay; so you have to add good light and writing tools and of course the absence of torture to make a prison serve.

You don't need much. I read once that a writer named Hinko Gottlieb, while in a German concentration camp, produced a novel, *The Key to the Great Gate*, that has been called "one of the most remarkable science fiction novels ever written." I don't know who said it. The book was written in Serbo-Croatian on toilet paper, to hide the manuscript from his German guards.

But anyplace can seem a prison. Théophile Gautier, author of *Mademoiselle de Maupin*, was locked by his father in an upstairs bedroom to complete his daily quota of words. He tried repeatedly to escape out the window, only to be dragged back to work. Is this peculiarly French? Colette was locked in her room by her husband, who then stole her work to publish under his own name.

Appealing workplaces are to be avoided. One wants a room with no view, so imagination can meet memory in the dark.

ANNIE DILLARD

I enjoy writing when I am in the desert. There are no distractions such as telephones, theatres, operas, houses and gardens.

AGATHA CHRISTIE

❊

An airplane or bus or train is an excellent place to write: you cannot leave. There is something about the gentle rocking motion of the enclosed vehicle that stimulates the Muse. I don't mean a short shuttle from D.C. up to New York City, but the long boring rides across all of Africa and up to Paris, or over Russia to India—long flights where hours of boredom and forced isolation invite the Muse to strike.

❊

Some writers actively seek discomfort and stress. Henry Miller would deliberately find an uncomfortable position in which to write. John Cheever daydreamed in his posthumously published journals about the perfect place and way to write:

> I sit at a large desk on which there is a polished brass stamp box, scales, paper weights, letter openers and so forth. On my right is a pile of clean yellow paper and on my left a pile of manuscript. I write in a small clear hand with a lead pencil and the words flow without interruption. As I watch myself I cover six or seven pages. My prose is somber and manly, the story I write is simple and compelling and nowhere eccentric. I seem to have recaptured the gift of narrative. I don't know what my subject is—love and death—but it is the extraordinary steadiness with which I work ... When I covered twelve or fifteen pages I ring a bell. A pleasant manservant enters with an ice bucket which he places on the bar. He then

A woman must have money and a room of her own if she is to write fiction.

VIRGINIA WOOLF

removes the manuscript. I pour four or five fingers of gin over some ice, flavor this with a little vermouth and walk around my warm and well-appointed study contentedly. It is a very large house.

A master in the art of living draws no sharp distinction between her work and her play, her labor and her leisure, her mind and her body, her education and her recreation. She hardly knows which is which. She simply pursues her vision of excellence through whatever she is doing and leaves others to determine whether she is working or playing. To herself she always seems to be doing both.

ANONYMOUS

I greatly admire the English writer, Henry Green . . . [He] wrote during the cocktail hour, the only time he could withdraw. Little by little he managed, in the cocktail hour, to produce a dozen novels.

CHRISTOPHER ISHERWOOD

WHEN AND HOW LONG

Gustave Flaubert worked sometimes from noon to four in the morning! He smoked fifteen pipes of tobacco during that sixteen-hour stint.

The very fact that he gives such hours as "times of writing" indicates the various definitions that different authors have for the work. Is "writing" creating the first draft? Revising? Editing and beginning again? First draft and the final comma inserted in the galleys all count. Each different phase of work brings its own emotional state.

⚛

Fyodor Dostoyevski wrote at night. William Faulkner claimed he wrote only when it rained.

Anthony Burgess writes in the afternoon, when, for him at least, "the unconscious mind has a habit of asserting itself."

Aldous Huxley put in three or four hours of writing before noon, and Tolstoy, Henry Miller and Thomas Mann likewise all preferred to write from 9:00 A.M. to 1:00 P.M.

If you are in difficulties with a book, try the element of surprise: attack it at an hour when it isn't expecting it.

H. G. WELLS

Be regular and orderly in your life like a bourgeois so that you may be violent and original in your work.

GUSTAVE FLAUBERT

I know writers who write only when inspiration comes. How would Isaac Stern play if he played the violin only when he felt like it? He would be lousy.

MADELEINE L'ENGLE

Flannery O'Connor, afflicted with lupus, could only write two hours a day—always at the same time, in the same place.

One friend, co-author of a bestseller and struggling with a book of her own, works during the "two or three hours when Lily is at childcare." Anne Tyler begins when she sends her children off to school and stops happily as soon as they come home.

The fact is, any time is a good time to write.

Tennessee Williams wrote at night if he was working by day, and by day if he had a night job.

❈

When I was youngly married and the new mother of a one-year-old, I fell into a depression. I found myself looking at the razor blades in the medicine cabinet (this was in Olden Times, when you actually bought double-sided sword-sharp blades). I shut the cabinet, appalled and frightened by my thoughts.

After that I forced myself awake at four-thirty in the morning to write for two hours before my husband and our baby woke up and the other duties of the day began.

The heart knows what it needs.

❈

Rainer Maria Rilke, the great German poet, described the artist's life, Cézanne's.

Only after forty did Cézanne, the Bohemian, give in to work—and then, says Rilke, he did nothing but work for the last years of his life.

> Without real pleasure it seems, in continual rage, ever at odds with his every endeavor, none of

One may go a long way after one is tired.

FRENCH PROVERB

If you wait for inspiration, you're not a writer, but a waiter.

ANONYMOUS

I work seven days a week, Sundays included. And I don't think it is a violation of the Sabbath. My only exception is Easter Sunday. It's a habit, an unbreakable habit. I don't know what I'd do if I didn't write. I'd probably go mad.

TENNESSEE WILLIAMS

which appeared to him to achieve what he regarded as the ultimate desirable. . . .

Old, ill, wearied every evening to the point of unconsciousness by the regularity of his daily work (so much so that he often went to bed at six o'clock as soon as it became dark after a supper mindlessly eaten), surly, mistrustful . . . he hoped from day to day still to attain that triumph . . . and does not know whether he has really succeeded. And sits in the garden like an old dog, the dog of this work which calls him again and again and beats him and lets him go hungry. And still he clings with all his strength to this incomprehensible master.

Easy reading is damned hard writing.

NATHANIEL HAWTHORNE

I have two methods of working. One of them involves tapping the sources of creativity. . . . I might be anywhere when it comes and I could end up writing all over the floor or up the walls and not knowing what is going on. It's like having a fit.

That either comes or it doesn't come.

The second method is following a trail made by my words themselves—by sitting down and writing . . . writing anything, fast. The words include the vision. That rush—that vision or high or whatever it is—doesn't last very long. A lot of writing gets done in a very short time, but it's not very good writing. Often it turns out to be just a reminder about how something felt. It has to be reworked.

MAXINE HONG KINGSTON

LETTING GO

Not long ago I met a man and his young blond pretty third wife who were collaborating on a novel. The wife is a sculptor and her bearded older husband a teacher. He has written nonfiction, but never a novel before. He said he hadn't started *writing* yet; he was still plotting, but he had an extensive outline. Now he knew what happened in every scene and soon he'd be able to begin. As he talked he made short, chopping motions with his right hand, slicing the air as if axing the head off his book. He had it totally under control.

He looked at me for approval.

I had none. *Mayday! Mayday!* I wanted to shout. *Right Brain! Let go!* Throw away everything you've done, I wanted to say. You're doing it wrong!

"Writing fiction is different from nonfiction," I said, choosing my words shyly. "Nonfiction, you're doing a crossword puzzle. It's color by number. You make an outline, flesh it in. Do more research. Write it down.

"But telling a story, you must trust your inner Self, let go of expectations, follow the story and see what the characters want to do.

Creativity is a continual surprise.

RAY BRADBURY

No one is more careful, more scrupulously honest, more devoted to his personal vision of the ideal, than a good professor trying to write a book about the Gilgamesh. *He may write far into the night, he may avoid parties, he may feel pangs of guilt about having spent too little time with his family. Nevertheless, his work is no more like an artist's work than the work of a first-class accountant is like that of an athlete contending for a championship. . . . No critical study, however brilliant, is the fierce psychological battle a novel is.*

JOHN GARDNER

The story chooses you, the image comes and then the emotional frame. You don't have a choice about writing the story. There's a filter at work which says this is or is not a story. . . . I think a story ideally comes to the writer; the writer shouldn't be casting the net out, searching for something to write about.

RAYMOND CARVER

"That's why writing fiction is so much fun. You're constantly surprised. Every day you get up and run to the desk to see what happens next."

I shut up then and let silence fall between us, as I considered how hard it is to trust the unknown. To let go of our handholds and free-fall into the unconscious, as deep as outer space. . . . The falling is a horrible sensation, when we're accustomed to clinging to control.

⊗

Tony Hillerman gave a talk in which he said he once made an outline for a book, "and wasted untold hours." Far better to make it up as you go along, as he did once when he tucked a dog into a particular chapter and found, pages later, the dog became important to the story.

⊗

Julia Cameron, who wrote *The Artist's Way*, begins each day with "Morning Pages"—three pages written as fast as possible without lifting the pen from the pad (yes, by hand); and in those Morning Pages she puts down whatever is on her mind or in her heart. . . . She tosses them unread into a knee-high pile and what matter if they never are seen by mortal eyes?

Now she begins to write.

⊗

Once I wrote a children's novel. It began when my ten-year-old daughter came to me one day and said, "Mom, I'm writing a story about a girl and her horse. Will you help me?"

In any work that is truly creative, I believe, the writer cannot be omniscient in advance about the effects that he proposes to produce. The suspense of a novel is not only in the reader, but in the novelist, who is intensely curious about what will happen to the hero.

MARY MCCARTHY

We do not write in order to be understood, we write in order to understand.

C. DAY-LEWIS

"Sure." I was flattered. An hour later I was pushing her away impatiently: "Go away, I'm writing your story." Poor child. It's no fun having a writer for a mother.

The story began as a simple tale about a little girl and her pony. I thought I knew what would happen: the untrained pony, the horse show, the victory—when suddenly at the end of five chapters the book shied. It wanted to take a fork in the path, bolt off in the wrong direction. I couldn't bring it under control. I left it finally and took up other work.

Two years later, I accidentally came across the manuscript. "This is really good!" I thought, and yet the problem was clear: the author had one story in mind, and the book wanted to tell another. Finally I decided to follow the lead to see where the book wanted to go. I could always go back if it didn't work (I told myself), and write out the story that I knew.

Every morning then I raced to the typewriter to see what happened next. I never knew from one sentence to the next what the characters would do. The book wrote itself with perfect structure, as if it already existed in an etheric template and waited only to be written down.

A few years later, writing a full-length, complex, adult novel, *Revelations*, the same thing happened. I planned an easy third-person omniscient author, when suddenly on page 10 a narrator appeared: an eighty-year-old man! I was horrified. I tried to kick him out. I'm not a man; I'm not eighty! For two months I stopped writing, fighting the narrator. In the end I buckled under angrily. I had to follow the rope of the story, hand over hand, blindly—curious about what was going on, always scared, but remembering that with that earlier novel the book knew its own plot. I flew on faith, reminding myself I could always go back if

Well, I don't know exactly how it's done. I let it alone a good deal.

SAUL BELLOW

Each time I write a book, every time I face that yellow pad, the challenge is so great. I have written eleven books, but each time I think, "Uh oh, they're going to find out now. I've run a game on everybody, and they're going to find me out."

MAYA ANGELOU

the story didn't work and with only a few years' work could cut the narrator out.

A year and a half later, when I came to the end of the novel (first draft: much more to go), I realized the story could not have been told without the narrator, would not have been as layered and rich. Our unconscious—the Muse—knows more than our conscious mind. Our business is to stay out of the way, stand back and then just watch the characters and write down what they say.

⚙

Not all writers are so vague. So, one writer plots her mysteries, but I like Walker Percy talking of the "knack" of writing a book, which is "a little trick one gets onto, a very minor trick." The novelist starts with himself as nothing and makes something of it, a matter that is possible, says Percy, only when he realizes the jig is up, all is lost, and all he can do is give up, let go.

⚙

How hard it is to trust! To know that you may spend a year on a book, or two, and give it up. Sometimes the story goes cold on you, the path fading into the underbrush until finally you lose the trail entirely. You are a bloodhound that has lost the scent and you wander in the scrub, round and round, desperate and guilty, and finally you stop baying and drag on home.

⚙

I heard once that Philip Roth worked a year on a book—and threw it away. It gave great comfort, though why I thought a year any length of time at all, I can't imagine now: everything I've written takes me years to complete.

Perhaps it would be better not to be a writer, but if you must, then write. If it all feels hopeless, if that famous "inspiration" will not come, write. If you are a genius, you'll make your own rules, but if not—and the odds are against it—go to your desk, no matter what your mood, face the icy challenge of the paper—write.

J. B. PRIESTLY

And whenever you begin a book—a story—you know that possibility exists that it won't work. Of course you never quite believe it, until one day you wake up and discover that months have passed, and somehow you let the project drop, and now you don't care about it anymore. . . . It's gone cold.

⚗

"Why do you write?" an author was asked at a cocktail party.

"I don't have anything better to do," she replied.

Only he who does nothing makes a mistake.

FRENCH PROVERB

When I want to read a good book, I write one.

BENJAMIN DISRAELI

MAKING
TIME

Tillie Olsen, in *Silences*, records the dark silences, the "unnatural thwarting of what wants to come into being, but cannot." There are so many: political upheavals, interruptions by children or the need to make a living, prejudice, fear, censorship, inertia and illness. . . . I bought the book when it first came out and often picked it up and put it down. I could not bear to read it, as if it would infect me with despair. There is *always* time, I tell myself, if I make it, if I claim it, if I want it enough. I repeat this like a mantra, stubbornly: I will *not* be pushed aside!

Benjamin Disraeli, the British prime minister, wrote novels. Winston Churchill won the Nobel Prize for his mastery of history and biographical description, especially concerning his six-volume history of the Second World War. I'm told Daniel Boorstin got up at 4:30 A.M. and wrote for several hours before going to work as head of the Library of Congress.

Writing is the only thing that . . . when I'm doing it, I don't feel that I should be doing something else instead.

GLORIA STEINEM

God has promised forgiveness to your repentence; but He has not promised tomorrow to your procrastination.

ST. AUGUSTINE

The only reward I look forward to is seeing the finished piece of writing in hand. And if I should find myself in a lazy spell, all I have to do to get active again is to remember how miserable life was for me when I was trying to get published.

ERSKINE CALDWELL

I used to wish on every star: let me be a writer. I prayed at night: help me write something good. I don't know where this urge came from, but I remember as a young woman sitting by the neighbor's pool in the summer, every fiber in my body held forcibly in place by courtesy; while inside I was screaming at the thought (I didn't know what to do with it then) of my waste of time, sitting in the sun; that there was something I was supposed to be doing, some place I was supposed to be! If only I knew what or where.

I have a lion inside me, and I have to feed it words every few days; when I don't, it begins to eat me instead.

❈

For seven years, Gerard Manley Hopkins, the poet-priest, kept a religious vow to refrain from writing poetry. In his last nine years he wrote only nineteen poems. "Time's eunuch," he wrote, "never to beget."

What waste! Of course to write, you write!

❈

I fret with impatience. Hurrying. I punish myself for working so slowly, for not going faster, doing more.

Then I remember that Michelangelo spent eight months with two workmen and his horse and without any other salary than his food, building the *road* up to the Carrara marble quarry, in order that he could cut a slab of the pure white stone that he needed to make the tomb that the egocentric Pope Julian II had commissioned for himself. What desperation did he feel, knowing he'd been banished to the road? And when he got back to Rome and learned that the Pope refused to see him—had changed his mind about the commission—how did he respond?

Life is very short and very uncertain; let us spend it as well as we can.

SAMUEL JOHNSON

I learned how to write in the interstices of daily life. . . .

MAXINE KUMIN

Michelangelo spent four years of furious solitary labor lying on his back painting the ceiling of the Sistine Chapel, paint falling in his eyes. For months afterward he could not read or look at drawings except with his head tilted back awkwardly. I think of earlier writers, preparing their tools. Would I have the patience to cut nibs on pens and grind oil, resin and colors for ink? Mix carbon and water-soluble resinous mediums, tannic acid, ferric sulfate and dyes? Would I have the patience to beat flax or papyrus into pulp, and then with more water pound it into a fleshy formless mat, as wool is matted into felt? Beating, carving, washing, smoothing, until I had a hundred sheets of paper on which to trace my words? Or would I have the means to buy the hide of a calf that an artisan had scraped at huge expense into soft enduring vellum? Could I wait so long to sing my song? And what would I write that would be worthy of such a costly surface?

I am filled with gratitude, to live as a woman at the end of the twentieth century in a country that permits my education and independence, a place and time where I can scrabble words onto the screen of my computer, and practice my art, where paper is cheap, and ink hardly even used, where I am permitted the luxury of writing—and even sometimes paid for it.

※

Once, driving in a car, the poet Anne Hobson Freeman asked me what I was most afraid of in life.

"Of not taking the dare!" I answered passionately.

"What dare?" she asked.

"I don't know! Whatever!" I cried, and tears of passion pricked my eyes. "Of getting to the end of my life and

I . . . have to constantly balance "being a writer" with being a wife and mother. It's a matter of putting two different things first, simultaneously.

MADELEINE L'ENGLE

Every book has been written with guilt, powered by pain. Every book has been a baby I did not bear, 10,000 meals I did not cook, 10,000 beds I did not make.

ERICA JONG

looking back and realizing I could have done it, and I didn't dare to risk."

The car moved on, past the pine trees, a dark gleaming green against a faultless sky. We blinked in the hard glittering autumn light. "What are you most afraid of?" I asked in return.

"Of being drowned in the minutiae of life," she answered quietly. "Of never having time to write."

"It's the same thing."

⊗

I remember when I was just starting as a writer, I had no experience. I didn't know that this is what a writer did— just *made* the time! All my earnings went for baby-sitters, while I prowled magazine offices, hunting an assignment, or else did library research or, counting my nickels, took the subway to interviews and later sat at my desk to write . . . a stream of sitters moving through the house. I lost money on the deal. No matter. I paid to learn, as other people pay for music lessons or to learn arithmetic.

I remember one day sitting at my desk in our bedroom (no room of my own: too poor). I stared at the paper in the typewriter, still blank, while outside the closed door my baby, my adorable Molly, screamed, pounding on the door. "MOMMY! MOMMY!" She wept hysterically, while the helpless sitter tried to pry her off the door. I sat at my desk, the tears running down my cheeks, convinced that if I let her in I would *never* write, would never be able to write, would never gain the space and time to myself that was needed to write; knowing too that I could not write then with my baby sobbing at the door, my hands shaking, my head spinning with the certainty that to give in was to give up, but that neither could I bear to hear her cry.

I shall live badly if I do not write, and I shall write badly if I do not live.

FRANÇOISE SAGAN

Walking on water wasn't built in a day.

JACK KEROUAC

"MOMMY!" she howled. "LET ME IN LET ME IN LET ME IN!" Eventually I did. It was exhausting for us both. Later I learned to concentrate with the baby paddling at my feet, just as she learned to play in innocent whispers, fearful of disturbing me.

A child is not a dog, to be trained to heel or sit. You learn to snatch ten minutes. You learn to write at night. Or at midday when the baby naps. . . . But I have also learned that nothing in this world has given me such pleasure as my children—no book or article or any prize has matched my pride at being the mother of my daughters; and at night in the shadow of my bed, alone now that they've grown, I think of Thoreau's wisdom when he said, "How can you sit down to write until you have stood up to live?"

※

One day when my children were still little, my husband's beautiful Aunt Becie telephoned. "I feel so old," I complained.

"Don't worry." She comforted me. "Soon the children will be grown and you'll be young again."

※

For the writer *time* is the most precious possession. Time to grow still. To reach this state, you sometimes go to a writers' colony.

Once there, it takes days to quiet your mind, to go deep and silent and true, drifting down into the dark pools of the unconscious mind, not speaking, not seeing, down, down, down like a sea turtle, silently into the mud of a meditative mind.

I know one newspaperman who went off to the

The solitude of writing is also quite frightening. It's quite close to madness, one just disappears for a day and loses touch.

NADINE GORDIMER

Writers don't write from experience, though many are resistant to admit that they don't. I want to be clear about this. If you wrote from experience, you'd get maybe one book, maybe three poems. Writers write from empathy.

NIKKI GIOVANNI

Whenever I have endured or accomplished some difficult task—such as watching television, going out socially or sleeping—I always look forward to rewarding myself with the small pleasure of getting back to my typewriter and writing something. This enables me to store up enough strength to endure the next interruption.

ISAAC ASIMOV

MacDowell Colony to write the Great American Novel. The isolation drove him mad. He bounced a basketball around his studio and snuck away to phone his wife, and when he returned to New York, he plunged back into the journalist's activity joyfully, the ambition of being a novelist quite killed.

I know another writer, an academic, who was given a prestigious grant to write a book. She took off a year without classes, set up an office in her basement and valiantly began. She used to call me. "What do you think of this sentence?" And "Listen to this transition." The second month she had a nervous breakdown, and then went back to the university that gave a structure to her days.

⚮

But oh, the gift of leisure! And oh, the limpid clarity of an empty mind! To be on a roll, writing effortlessly . . . And oh, the pain of being forced out of the writer's trance before it's done. Your children come home. Or you have to cook dinner, or answer the phone, or go to your job or to the dinner party that you stupidly accepted three weeks earlier, when you had no idea you'd be writing well that day. You jerk out of the embrace of the Muse with all the pain of coitus interruptus—and no sympathy from those nearby who do not know that elegant space or the gift of long lazy leisurely uninterrupted hours of a day.

They look at you in amazement: the life of a mole. Some try to bring you out of your boredom, out into the "world." To go to the theater, perhaps, or socialize . . .

⚮

I will say this: no loneliness or solitude matches the fatigue and awful lonesomeness that comes in crowds or in

*I feel that art has something to do with the achievement of still-
ness in the midst of chaos. A stillness which characterizes
prayer, too, and the eye of the storm. I think that art has something to do with an arrest of attention in the midst of distrac-
tion.*

SAUL BELLOW

continually being available to others at the expense of your inner voice. Musicians feel it too. Gian Carlo Menotti says that's why he has a place in Scotland, where silence is inexpensive, because what musicians want is not music but silence in which to listen. The loneliness of artistic creation, after all, is momentary, because the act of creating creates that perfect unity when Time stands still and you experience only stillness, and in utter emptiness the fullness of your Self.

What! Another damned, thick, square book! Always scribble,
scribble, scribble, eh, Mr. Gibbon!

WILLIAM HENRY, DUKE OF GLOUCESTER,
TO EDWARD GIBBON, 1781

I love writing. It's the paperwork that gets me.

PETER DE VRIES

My whole interest is in the act of writing itself.

JOHN FOWLES

PRODUCTIVITY

Most writers find they can write for three or four hours at a stretch when composing new material, though they can correct and edit for twice that long. Occasionally we read of an author—John Fowles, for example—who works twelve to fourteen hours in a kind of drunken trance.

※

Jack London worked sixteen to eighteen hours a day, writing in the same frenzy with which he lived. He wrote fifty books in sixteen years. Then at the age of forty he killed himself.

※

The Nobel laureate Gabriel García Márquez told an interviewer in 1973 that the first chapter of *One Hundred Years of Solitude* came like a flash from the blue as he was driving to Acapulco. He returned to his home in Mexico City, barricaded himself in his room, and wrote the book in eighteen months of ten-hour days.

"When I was finished writing, my wife said, 'Did you finish it? We owe twelve thousand dollars.' "

※

I seem to have a finite amount of new or first-draft writing

There are three rules for writing a novel. Unfortunately no one knows what they are.

W. SOMERSET MAUGHAM

The best time for planning a book is while you're doing the dishes.

AGATHA CHRISTIE

that can be done in any week. If on Monday I write twice my usual quota, Tuesday will be dry. If I write like a fury, accomplishing in three days what usually takes seven—no more will come to my hand in the following four days, though I sit for hours, constipated, at my desk. The well is dry. How jealous I am of those endless bubbling springs!

I console myself, hoarding facts about other writers: John Cheever, who wrote continuously for fifty years, published one hundred twenty short stories in *The New Yorker*. Do the math. It comes to only 2.4 a year!

The ones he liked best were those he finished in a single week.

⊗

Émile Zola sat ten hours a day at his desk. Much of this time was spent staring out the window in a brooding effort to call up a certain scene. It was work. Zola claimed that at times the struggle with a certain passage was so intense it caused an erection.

But sitting ten hours is hard on the back. Another writer walks. "Three miles a page," he says.

⊗

"I am a galley slave to pen and ink," wrote Honoré de Balzac, who produced his vast output working nonstop in sixteen-hour stretches.

We are reminded of Agatha Christie, who could finish a book in six weeks using three fingers on the typewriter. "A sausage machine," she called herself. "A perfect sausage machine." She wrote eighty-three crime novels in fifty-six years, six romantic novels under the name of Mary Westmacott, not to mention plays. And it was not that she had no other duties. In the six years of World War II,

La Genie, c'est travailler tous les jours.

GUSTAVE FLAUBERT

All art is a kind of confession.

JAMES BALDWIN

The more a man writes, the more he can write.

WILLIAM HAZLITT

when she held a full-time job in a hospital, she wrote twelve books.

※

It's discouraging. Just when you think you've heard the record—hit the wall—for productivity, you hear of another breakthrough.

Zane Grey wrote fifty-four novels about the Old West, Manfred B. Lee and Frederic Dannay some forty Ellery Queen mysteries. Isaac Asimov, who wrote every day of his adult life from dawn to dusk, until his death at seventy-two, produced almost four hundred books—everything from science fact and science fiction to Shakespeare and dirty limericks. . . .

※

Genre writers in particular produce gargantuan amounts. Barbara Cartland, whose sales have topped $100 million, takes two or three weeks to complete a book, and fourteen times she set the world record for annual output with an average of twenty-three books a year: twenty novels in 1975, twenty-one in 1976, twenty-four in 1977. She published over 515 novels with fifty million copies sold around the world. When she was ninety years old in 1991, she was still bringing out a book a month.

※

Anthony Trollope wrote three hours a day, every day, by the clock. And this was by pen! He wrote two hundred and fifty words every fifteen minutes, and if by checking his watch he found himself behind, he hurried to make up his thousand words an hour, three thousand words each day. At two hundred words a page, let's say, that comes to

One of the marks of true genius is a quality of abundance. A rich, rollicking abundance, enough to give indigestion to ordinary people.

CATHERINE DRINKER BOWEN

A writer's job is to imagine everything so personally that the fiction is as vivid as memories.

JOHN IRVING

fifteen pages a day, one hundred pages every week, or more. Then he went to his office, to work.

How could he sustain that level? When did he rewrite, which is what most writers do?

※

George Sand wrote seven plays and almost fifty books—including a four-volume autobiography—using, what? A quill! For a time she published her own newspaper—and in addition she married, traveled, took lovers, bore and reared children and watched some die. In some periods she published two and three books a year.

※

Georges Simenon, the French detective writer, produced two Inspector Maigret novels a *month* for two years. It took an average of eleven days to finish one, though he once completed a short Maigret novel in one nonstop feverish twenty-four-hour gulp.

He wrote one hundred and fifty novels under his best-known pseudonym, Simenon, and some three hundred and fifty others under different names.

But Simenon, born Georges Sim, took his writing seriously. Before beginning a major work, he had a checkup by his doctor, received permission to work, then holed himself up in his room. He took no phone calls, saw no one, answered no mail, and ate the meals his housekeeper (also his mistress) left outside his door. At the end of six weeks, he staggered back to the outside world, physically ill, depleted, but with another volume done. Between these workaholic writing binges, he indulged his sexual appetites, sometimes with five prostitutes in a single day.

All a man has to do is get a woman to say he's a writer; it's an aphrodisiac.

SAUL BELLOW

The sum which two married people owe to one another defies calculation. It is an infinite debt, which can only be discharged through all eternity.

JOHANN WOLFGANG GOETHE

Later, he wrote in his autobiography of having violated his daughter as well, sex and creativity perversely intertwined.

※

Creativity and sex are known to be intimately linked, as are creativity and love—except I don't know how. One woman writer loses all sexual interest when working on a book, as if all her energy becomes too tightly focused. But when it is finished, she walks down the street looking hungrily at men, sexuality flaring off her skin. One man, on the other hand, tells me that intercourse stimulates his creativity, that his work is enhanced by sex. He does not bond in these encounters, as the woman might, but dodges in and out as if engaged in guerrilla warfare.

This is different from romantic love, with its veering heights and falls, and different also from the steady, sweet creative urgency of love returned. Samuel Clemens, who wrote as Mark Twain, put down his pen upon the death of his beloved wife and never wrote another word.

※

Virginia Woolf was protected from sex both by her sister, Vanessa, and her husband, Leonard Woolf. Leonard was Virginia's best friend, and her editor and publisher as well as her husband, and he felt Virginia was too frail for sex, though possibly he meant for the children that result from it. She'd already had plenty of childhood sexual abuse, and a history of mental instability. No wonder she fell in love with Vita Sackville-West, wrote passionately of women's history, insisting on a radical rewriting of the history of men! No wonder, too, she was envious of her sister for having children. Virginia took them on outings, to buy them shoes. . . .

I've never possessed either facility in conception or in expression. It should be self-evident that the small amount of work I've produced has been the result of long and painful labour . . . labour by which a revery becomes a work of art.

CHARLES BAUDELAIRE

Yesterday for the first time in months, an indisputable ability to do good work. And yet wrote only the first page. Again I realize that everything written down bit by bit rather than all at once in the course of the larger part is inferior, and that the circumstances of my life condemn me to this inferiority.

FRANZ KAFKA

Of course the question remains: would she have written what she did if she'd had children and known good sex? And would she have drowned herself, walking into the River Ouse, a large stone in the pocket of her coat? Did any of it have to do with sex?

※

But I was talking about productivity, and the abundance that rolls from some creators and the controlled and restrictive anorexia of others; and it might be mentioned that some writers have balance in their lives. Not all writers work at fever pitch, damaging thier bodies with drugs and overwork; and neither should we confuse quantity with quality of work. Franz Kafka, who worked as an official in an insurance agency and wrote when he could, agonized over every word.

Donald Hall, one of the country's most extensively published poets, a former Guggenheim fellow and past poetry editor of the *Paris Review*, explained in one newspaper interview that his customary turnaround time—the interval between conception of an idea and publication of the poem—is "three to five years." The late Philip Larkin, former Poet Laureate, wrote at his own estimation three poems a year.

Forcing oneself into producing certain kinds of work can dry up productivity almost completely. The short story writer Katherine Anne Porter, at the prodding of her editor to undertake the longer form, took twenty years to write the novel *Ship of Fools*.

John Updike does his three pages a day, slow and steady.

Hemingway kept a chart of his progress on a huge piece of cardboard "so as not to kid myself." He wrote four

You don't know what it is to stay a whole day with your head in your hands trying to squeeze your unfortunate brain so as to find a word. Ah! I know the agonies of style

GUSTAVE FLAUBERT,
WRITING TO GEORGE SAND

When you write, you lay out a line of words. The line of words is a miner's pick, a woodcarver's gouge, a surgeon's probe. You wield it, and it digs a path you follow. Soon you find yourself deep in new territory. Is it a dead end, or have you located the real subject? You will know tomorrow, or this time next year.

ANNIE DILLARD

hundred and fifty to six hundred words a day—less than two pages, not much more than three—working assiduously, I'm told, four hours a day. I don't know if this was before his talents were destroyed by alcohol, or whether his output grew smaller once he started in to full-time drink.

Judith Viorst set herself the task of writing for one novel one publishable page a day, two hundred and eighty words, slow and steady, one chapter a month. She could get ahead but never fall behind. If she got ahead, she could take a day off. And this she did, writing some months on and some months off until the book was done. Judith used to write for a newspaper. Her editor there told me she was the only writer who turned in perfect copy, not a comma out of place.

※

It takes time, sometimes, to fill the well. Mostly it takes time to be big enough to have anything to say. Cormac McCarthy, whose magnificent *All the Pretty Horses* came out in 1992, published his first novel in 1965. In twenty-seven years he has written five good books.

William Styron is another author who proceeds slowly in his work.

I comfort myself with comparisons like these. In the early 1700s, the Neapolitan Giovanni Battista Vico changed the very study of history. He lived in squalor, obsessed by his worthless book, writing, rewriting for twenty years, while his poor wife nagged and wept and tried to feed the dozens of children he gave her. His work, *La Scienza Nuova*, was practically unknown in his lifetime. Vico never knew that this one work changed the course of intellectual history, establishing the concept of repeated patterns or the circularity of history.

I work continuously within the shadow of failure. For every novel that makes it to my publisher's desk, there are at least five or six that died on the way.

GAIL GODWIN

We look back now and ask from the comfortable distance of our own century— Was his life a failure or success? By what standard do we measure him?

☒

Gustave Flaubert wrote so painfully that he could spend five days, he lamented to his mistress, on a single paragraph! But now we are into rewriting, which is what most writers do.

First drafts are for learning what your novel or story is about.
BERNARD MALAMUD

This morning I took the hyphen out of Hell-hound and this afternoon I put it back.
EDWIN ARLINGTON ROBINSON

The essays were a tremendous struggle. Each of the large ones took nine months to a year. I've had thousands of pages for a 30-page essay—30 or 40 drafts of every page. "On Photography," which is six essays, took five years. And I mean working every single day. . . . Just writing. I'd get started, and then I'd run into a ditch, and then I would start again—and again.
SUSAN SONTAG

REWRITING

Sometimes I think that writing is no more than rewriting, and then I scold myself that I cannot let a thing go, but keep on working and fretting it, until one day I wake up and say, "It's done." After that the words cannot be changed. But before that point there is only work.

I get discouraged at the constancy of revising. I get annoyed that I can't, like Anita Brookner, just put it down the first time and have it come out right—"no drafts, no fetishes, no false starts," she wrote, "there simply isn't *time*." I get discouraged, and yet what else is writing but trial and error? Moreover, many times I have written whole chapters and revised, only to find the words insisted on going back to that first draft, and then no matter how much revising I do, how much editing, those were the first and perfect words, those rhythms, engraved in Time.

⊗

The finer the material, as a general rule, the more it has been smoothed to arrive at its final stage. Raymond Carver said that if his first draft of a story was around forty pages, it would be half that by the time he was through, adding and editing, and loving the process of "putting words in and taking words out."

Much of the stuff which I will finally publish, with all its flaws, as if it had been dashed off with a felt pen, will have begun eight or more years earlier, and worried and slowly chewed on and left for dead many times in the interim.

WILLIAM GASS

I thought of "Lycidas" as a full-grown beauty—as springing up with all its parts absolute—till, in an evil hour, I was shown the original copy of it in the library of Trinity, kept like treasure to be proud of. I wish they had thrown them into the Cam, or sent them into the Irish Channel. How it staggered me to see the fine things in their ore! Interlined, corrected! as if their words were mortal, alterable, displaceable at pleasure! as if they might have been otherwise and just as good! as if inspiration were made up of parts, and these fluctuating, successive, indifferent! I will never go into the work shop of any great artist again.

CHARLES LAMB

❈

Publishers are aware of this dissatisfaction in authors and often, to hold them in check, insert a clause in the contract that forces the writer to pay for any galley changes past a certain minimal amount.

❈

It takes courage. D. H. Lawrence, who wrote ten novels in his twenty-year career—and plays, short stories, poetry, essays—was working on a book called *The Two Sisters*. He rewrote it several times, then decided to throw out a thousand pages that he'd done and make them into two books. They became *Women in Love* and *The Rainbow*.

❈

I have a friend, John Greenya, who has written and ghostwritten over a dozen books of true crime and law. He tells how a young writer came to him once asking advice on his treasured manuscript. John read it carefully. "If you're going to be a writer," he told him, "the proof will be in the rewriting. You have to make it a real story." And he talked him through the work.

"Gotcha," the young man kept saying. "Gotcha."

A week later, he came back. "I've made all the changes you wanted," he said.

"I knew he wouldn't be a writer," said John. "It should have taken him three to six months. He wanted to call himself a writer. But he didn't want to do the work."

❈

I have heard that an eagle misses seventy percent of its strikes. Why should I expect to do better? And when he

To be a writer is to throw away a great deal, not to be satisfied, to type again, and then again and once more, and over and over.

JOHN HERSEY

I have often rewritten—often several times—every word I have ever published. My pencils outlast their erasers.

VLADIMIR NABOKOV

misses, does he scold himself, I wonder, for failing at the task?

❀

Sometimes you have changed. You put aside a book for a year or five and when you return to it you see only changes to be made. You've changed. It must be changed.

John Fowles did not publish *The Magus*, the first novel he had attempted, until 1966. He was forty by then. He had been writing for more than ten years and had published other work. Twelve years later, in 1978, he published a revised version of *The Magus*. He could not stop rewriting it.

Walt Whitman spent his lifetime rewriting *Leaves of Grass*, his celebration of sexuality and life. The last edition came out when he was seventy-three, just before his death.

In the end, all books are written for your friends.

GABRIEL GARCÍA MÁRQUEZ

Each of us is like a desert, and a literary work is like a cry from the desert, or like a pigeon let loose with a message in its claws, or like a bottle thrown into the sea. The point is: to be heard—even if by one single person.

FRANÇOIS MAURIAC

Audience

Long before she published even a magazine article, one writer I know wrote a little book as a present for a favorite sister-in-law. She wrote it by hand in fine calligraphy, and the first capital letter of each chapter was set off in a box, as in an illuminated manuscript, and intertwined with painted animals and vines. Animals and vines lovingly embraced the letters, so full was her heart with love of words and longing to have them read by other eyes.

⚘

I once met a sculptor who will not sell or give away her work. She needs her pieces around her. "They are my children," she says. "I can't part with them."

But others need audience. For them, the work is not complete until it's been received. Like a three-legged stool formed of artist-object-reader, the work requires the viewer or reader, who will carry it away with him.

⚘

Once, walking down Sixth Avenue in New York, just at the CBS Building, I came to a man hawking chapters from his novel. He had a box on the ledge beside him and in it were the neatly typed pages of his book, on white bond paper, with the proper one-inch margins all around and each chapter paper-clipped—or was it stapled? I don't re-

I would rather be attacked than unnoticed. For the worst thing you can do to an author is to be silent as to his works.

SAMUEL JOHNSON

Any writer overwhelmingly honest about pleasing himself is almost sure to please others.

MARIANNE MOORE

member. What I remember was the author standing a little angrily on the sidewalk, holding aloft a dozen fluttering manuscript pages, as he called out his wares: fifty cents a chapter to any passerby. I stopped and browsed through a chapter, touched and frightened by his hurt determination, and by the raspberry he gave with this act to rejecting publishers, and touched also by his courage: he insisted on an audience!

I didn't buy a chapter. I wish I had. I wish I'd bought the whole book, cheap at the price, but instead I walked on, troubled at my own work's fate. I remembered how in ancient Rome the poets would likewise stand on the street corners, shouting their verses at the top of their lungs, over the thunder of iron wagon wheels on cobblestones, the cries of fruit and vegetable hawkers, or the screaming of other poets on other corners, not to mention the general jostle and bustle and noise of indifferent crowds.

⊗

A friend of mine is founder and editor of a small publishing house in Maine. One year he published what he calls "poems by crazy people"—a small volume of poems by mentally ill and retarded men and women in his area. Their response to success astonished him. One of the poets took a job. Another man, so troubled he could hardly form his words, stood up before an audience and read his poems aloud. And a woman, holding the book to her heart, said passionately: "Now I have something for my children to remember me by."

The remark filled my friend with terrible, poignant sorrow—lest the woman felt her children would not otherwise remember her, lest she give too much importance to publication.

Why I write. Of course I stole the title for this talk from George Orwell. One reason I stole it was that I like the sound of the words: Why I write. *There you have three short unambiguous words that share a sound, and the sound they share is this:*

I

I

I

JOAN DIDION

A person who publishes a book willfully appears before the populace with his pants down. . . . If it is a good book nothing can hurt him. If it is a bad book nothing can help him.

EDNA ST. VINCENT MILLAY

Yet, I understand the sense of achievement and accomplishment she felt, and with it the self-esteem, as if now the Self is validated. You have yelled out to the Universe the lonely vowels, I-I-I-I-I, and heard them echo back a whispered ... "Yes, you *are*. . . ."

⋈

The druids held that to commit their sacred doctrines to writing would be to desecrate them, and Emily Dickinson felt publication formed no part of a poet's business. Only two of her poems were published in her lifetime, and neither by her consent. Publication, she wrote contemptuously, "is the auction of the Mind of Man." But most writers want to be heard, especially by their peers, and publication remains the usual means these days.

⋈

What we want is acceptance, appreciation. In the sixteenth century, Edmund Spenser took his long poem *The Faerie Queene* to Sir Philip Sidney, in hopes of attracting a patron who would so admire the work that he would pay the poet and help him to live another day to write another work. . . .

"Sir Philip was busy at his Study," writes Spenser's biographer, John Aubrey, "and his servant delivered Mr. Spenser's book to his master, who laid it by, thinking it might be such kind of Stuffe as he was frequently troubled with. Mr. Spencer [sic] stayed so long that his patience was wearied, and went his way discontented, and never intended to come again. When Sir Philip

I write very personal poems but I hope that they will become the central theme to someone else's private life.

ANNE SEXTON

Only connect.

E. M. FORSTER

perused it, he was so exceedingly delighted with it that he was extremely sorry he was gone, and where to send for him he knew not. After much enquiry he learned his lodging, and sent for him, mightily caressed him, and ordered his servant to give him so many pounds in gold. His servant sayd that that was too much. No, sayd Sir Philip, and ordered an addition. From this time there was a great friendship between them, to his dying day."

And that is what we want in a publisher, an approving audience—the gift received.

※

Success itself brings loss, an agonizing readjustment of self. For ten years, from the ages of twenty-five to thirty-five, Margaret Mitchell worked on *Gone with the Wind*. Like Jane Austen, she wrote it secretly, hiding the manuscript's existence even from her friends. Indeed, she showed it to an editor only because one came to Atlanta hunting for new talent, and shyly she allowed him to read her work. After it was published, Mitchell never wrote another book, so stunned was she by her celebrity and success. Thirteen years later she was killed by a taxi while crossing an Atlanta street.

Flaubert condemned the success of *Madame Bovary*, which brought him both lawsuits for obscenity and attempted censorship. Thomas Hardy was so disillusioned by the scandal and success engendered by his realistic novels that he quit, to write poetry for the rest of his life.

※

For myself, I want an audience: I want my work, my chil-

Not to have audience is a kind of death.

TILLIE OLSEN

There is only one real deprivation, I decided this morning, and that is not to be able to give one's gift to those one loves most. The gift turned inward, unable to be given, becomes a heavy burden, even sometimes a kind of poison. It is as though the flow of life were backed up.

MAY SARTON

dren, received. But I have learned I cannot ask for that.

One year, in 1988, I gave up writing. The decision did not come easily. For eight years in a frenzy of creativity, I had been writing full-time, obsessively, compulsively: novels, plays, nonfiction. It had been ten years since I had published a book. I felt I had failed.

One night I drove up to the Washington National Cathedral, where the Chapel of the Good Shepherd stood open—at that time, all night. This is a tiny chapel, hardly big enough for three people. It was ten-thirty at night. I didn't kneel. I threw myself full out on the black stone floor, crying out my anguish to God.

I felt as if I had worked with all my heart and mind and soul and strength, and my efforts had not been received. I felt worthless, bereft.

I lay on the floor of the chapel, weeping and praying for understanding and relief, when footsteps sounded on the stones. Quickly I scrambled to my feet and wiped away the tears.

A young woman entered. It turned out she was an artist, and we began to talk about work.

She reminded me that we cannot ask for recognition. It's not the artist's place. All we can do is work with all our hearts. What happens is not our responsibility.

I went away marveling at this curious and coincidental encounter with the golden-haired girl. She was not an angel; I have seen her since. But she came that night auspiciously to deliver the message that I needed to hear.

I went away consoled. Nonetheless, I decided to give up writing. I'd been a writer for more than twenty years, I told myself. I didn't need to do it anymore. I would get a job, I told myself, work in an office nine to five like ordinary people. (Actually I discovered I was unemployable

For a self is a thing the world is least apt to inquire about, and the thing of all things the most dangerous for a man to let people notice that he has. The greatest danger, that of losing one's own self, may pass off as quietly as if it were nothing; every other loss, that of an arm, a leg, five dollars, a wife, etc., is sure to be noticed.

SØREN KIERKEGAARD

I don't have a sense of a so-called ideal reader and certainly not of a readership, that terrific entity. I write for the page.

DON DELILLO

Writing is a form of therapy; sometimes I wonder how all those who do not write, compose or paint can manage to escape the madness, the melancholia, the panic fear which is inherent in a human situation.

GRAHAM GREENE

and found no job.) All year I wrote nothing more interesting than a résumé; yet that was the year I made more money from my writing than ever before. Essays published years before were suddenly syndicated in countries all around the world; an early novel, long out of print, was unexpectedly optioned for a film; and finally one of the books written in that long dry period found its publisher. I laughed about it. It was as if once I let go of my longing for an outcome, God could turn his attention from the Middle East: "Oh, wait, you want to be a writer. Here!"

But first I had to find a self beyond my work.

⊗

Is the lesson about letting go? Certainly it applies to creating itself. You work until your fingers bleed. You falter from depression and despair—give up—and only then the flash of insight comes, a bolt from the blue. When you're thinking of something else. Is it a law of the universe? Work, let go?

⊗

We write to expiate and extirpate our shame and guilt and anger and grief and loneliness and impotence. We write at the injustice of the world. We write in order to create order out of chaos, reordering it over and over, in terror that the chaos may indeed be meaningless. We write to uncover our deepest secrets to ourselves, to understand. We write in an outpouring of love.

We write in secret, either for publication or for a journal no one will see, or we write poems to be privately printed for the eyes of friends alone—this is not our choice. The urge is to create. The outcome belongs to God.

Anything we fully do is an alone journey.

NATALIE GOLDBERG

As a writer you are free. You are about the freest person that ever was. Your freedom is what you have bought with your solitude, your loneliness.

URSULA K. LE GUIN

ALONENESS

I look at my love affair with this writing and wonder at its power. It's not that I'm so productive or even so fine a writer, but *driven* ... nothing gets in the way of these demands—not marriage, not the put-downs of other people, not poverty, not even the sedition of self-doubt.

This work requires independence. I like Beryl Markham, flying her own airplane around East Africa, not caring (I make up the script) what others thought or how she ought to write. I like Anne Sexton and Maxine Kumin writing their fierce poetry, and I like the unmarried Dorothy Sayers becoming pregnant (a sin) and later pouring out her love on a man "incapable of receiving it," to use Carolyn Heilbrun's words; and thus ensuring for herself both love and freedom; which means time to do her work.

One of the hardest things for me has been the absence of role models. Men. Women. Especially the women. Where were the women artists of an earlier generation? Where were the writers known to me personally—neighbors, friends, mothers of children, artists, cohorts who could lead me on the path?

The fact is they were everywhere around, fighting their own lonely battles.

I didn't know them.

Also I didn't know that if I did know them it would

The price for living the life I have—for any serious, devoted person, is that at times one must live alone, or feel alone. I think loneliness is associated in many people's minds when they think about success.

HELEN FRANKENTHALER

I was always my own teacher.

EUDORA WELTY

Poetry does not feed, but men have died for want of it.

ROBERT F. KENNEDY

have made no difference. We are all explorers on this path, alone, whacking the bushes with our blunt machetes and swiping sweat out of our eyes and the glue-legged flies from off our sticky skin. Always alone, putting one foot before the next on this adventure, always in uncharted territory, and no guide or role model in the world to help with the work, because even if an earlier writer had worked here before, she leaves no tracks. In writing—in creating any art—you are doing one of two things. Either you are walking naked at the edge of a lunar landscape, small and lonely against the far-off stars, or else you're following pitifully in someone else's tracks. Not exploring. Not hurting. Not creating something never done before. No. A role model, a guide could do no more than say—"Go on! Let's see if you've got the grit to do the job. Challenge the universe." She would say—"Dare the demons to keep you from the cave of gold, and if you die in the jungle out there, bones moldering, not found for centuries, if ever found at all by another adventurer stumbling on them unawares—if you die, well, so what? At least you did the best you could."

So you hack at the jungle foliage, knowing only that others have come this way before . . . sometime . . . and left no trails. . . .

Modern poets talk against business, poor things, but all of us write for money. Beginners are subjected to trial by pocket, poor things.

ROBERT FROST

Almost anyone can be an author; the business is to collect money and fame from this state of being.

A. A. MILNE

MONEY

And then there is money. I think that at some level all writers (okay, except Emily Dickinson) expect to be paid for their work. That's because no one can imagine that what is so compelling to her, or him, is not worth money to someone else.

On the other hand, the good writer does not confuse his desire to be paid with the obsession to write. It is the compulsion that brings both joy and pain. Occasionally it brings the means to be paid.

⚯

"No man but a blockhead ever wrote except for money," said Samuel Johnson, thus condemning the majority of writers, musicians, composers, and artists. If writers followed his instructions, the world would be a lesser place, deprived of our poets. Dr. Johnson would have been deprived of his adoring biographer, James Boswell, as well. But perhaps in an attempt to shield himself from derision, or perhaps in acknowledgment of his need for his admirer, Johnson also said, "The applause of a single human being is of great consequence."

A writer writes for many reasons, money being only one.

Whatever money or praise comes from writing seems totally unreal to me. The money always seems like play money or found money, totally unrelated to the writing that brought it. The praise or criticism always seems like it's being said not about me but about someone I don't know, a stranger.

HARRY CREWS

No one made you become a playwright.

ROBERT ANDERSON

∞

Walt Whitman lost money on the first edition of *Leaves of Grass*. Ezra Pound's American royalties for a typical year—1915—came to $1.85.

Many writers are supported by a full-time working spouse. During the Depression, Isaac Bashevis Singer's wife worked in a factory sewing sweatbands into hats while he wrote in Yiddish for the *Jewish Daily Forward*.

Students ask, "What is the most important thing a writer needs?" and without hesitation the author responds, "An independent income."

Each year, some 45,000 books are published in the United States, 3,750 books a month—cookbooks, romance novels, mysteries, how-to's, and even a few works of literature. One Author's Guild survey showed that the median income from writing is $5,000 a year.

∞

I have written articles that paid less than the expenses. And been grateful for the chance. All starting writers have to write "on spec" (speculation) or agree to payment on publication instead of on acceptance (and who knows in how many years the magazine will decide to publish it—if ever); and all writers, no matter their prestige, are subject to the whims and malice of publishers' bookkeepers balancing their books by withholding the writers' fees: six months in arrears is the usual "float."

"Writers are the, excuse my language, n-i-g-g-e-r-s of this profession," said Les Whitten to me one day. Les is in my writers' group that meets for lunch once a month. Author of twelve books, Les was at that time in a trough, un-

I never had any doubts about my abilities. I knew I could write. I just had to figure out how to eat while doing this.

CORMAC MCCARTHY

Anyone who has a choice and doesn't choose not *to write is a fool. . . . The work is hard, the perks are few, the pay is terrible, and the product, when it's finally finished, is pure joy.*

MARY LEE SETTLE

able to find a home for his latest and most ambitious work. He knew what he was speaking of. So did we.

※

"Isn't it wonderful!" said the publisher to the writer. "A bestseller! You'll make twenty thousand dollars." This was in the early 1970s, when a dollar was worth more than two of today's.

"Yes," said the writer, "but I figure it cost me forty-three thousand, five hundred dollars, to write the book. Assuming that I could have found a job for twelve thousand dollars a year—that's not much . . . and three years of working on the book . . . thirty-six thousand dollars, and then expenses . . ."

It makes you angry, this constant fight for what is yours, the demeaning, degrading need to call an editor and beg for your money, the wasted energy that could be spent on writing, while instead you scurry in anxiety to find the means to pay the bills! In the end you grit your teeth and accept. . . .

It's the price you pay for doing what you love . . . and yet no different from the life of an actor, struggling for a break, or a painter working decades without remuneration because nothing else is worth it but to paint . . . or a cabinetmaker, because he loves the feel of wood.

Writers have a little holy light within, like a pilot light which fear is always blowing out. When a writer brings a manuscript fresh from the making, at the moment of greatest vulnerability, that's the moment for friends to help get the little holy light lit again.

CYNTHIA OZICK

The profession of book-writing makes horse racing seem like a solid, stable business.

JOHN STEINBECK

REJECTION

A writer lives with rejection. First there is self-rejection. No matter how frequently you are published, you suffer doubt and loneliness and fear.

Then there is the rejection of others.

A writer needs the sensitivity of a butterfly in touching the outside world—and the skin of a rhino to withstand its disregard.

Iris Murdoch, who made her debut as a writer in 1954, wrote three novels before she got one published. Since the 1960s she has published almost a book a year, reaching twenty-four in all, not counting works of philosophy.

The publishing world is full of bestsellers that were read and rejected in manuscript. Some of these stories are told by the editors themselves, drinking away their remorse. Robert Pirsig received 121 rejections, he says, before *Zen and the Art of Motorcycle Maintenance* was accepted for publication. *Jonathan Livingston Seagull* circulated to forty publishers. Norman Mailer's *The Naked and the Dead* went to eleven publishers before the twelfth dared accept it. Joseph Heller's classic *Catch-22*, William Kennedy's *Ironweed*, Erich Segal's *Love Story*, Tom Clancy's *The Hunt for Red October*, *The Diary of Anne Frank*, or M. Scott Peck's *The Road Less Traveled* . . . so many manuscripts circulating valiantly to one publisher after another before rushing off to stardom and maybe movie rights.

As a man who has knocked about the arts for some time, I can only say that in the presence of a poet I am struck with awe that I should behold so courageous a man. I never felt that way about generals or admirals, for our society is organized to protect the warrior.

JAMES A. MICHENER

Whenever one of us got an A or even a strong B+ we would instantly, with a wild and nutty gambler's optimism, whip that story off to The New Yorker. *We could have papered our rooms with those politely printed form rejection slips.*

ALICE ADAMS

⊗

Beatrix Potter's Peter Rabbit books were turned down so often that she finally published them herself. Not to mention Virginia Woolf's privately printed works. My favorite image is of Emily Brontë, sending out her novel, *Wuthering Heights*, to one rejecting publisher after another, each time packing it defiantly in the very envelope it had just been returned in, so the next publisher could read the list of rival houses that had already refused the manuscript. I'm not sure I'd have the courage to put an editor to that test.

Victor Villaseñor, author of *Rain of Gold*, wrote nine novels and sixty-five short stories, earning 265 rejections before he sold his novel *Macho!* in 1970.

The first book of Margaret Chittenden, a writer of children's books, was turned down by twenty-five publishers before finding a home. John Creasey, an English mystery writer, collected 743 rejections before selling a single book. He went on to write six hundred books under twenty-eight pseudonyms.

⊗

Truman Capote says that "no writers ever forget their first acceptance." But this is because at the age of seventeen he received three acceptance letters on the same day for his short stories.

What I clearly remember is my first rejection. I stood in the little front hall of our first apartment, beside the red velvet sofa, leafing through the mail. In it was a preprinted postcard from *The Atlantic Monthly*. (What did I know, twenty-five years old, about how or where to send a short story?) I read the rejection. My heart flew up with

We can secure other people's approval if we do right and try hard; but our own is worth a hundred of it, and no way has been found of securing that.

MARK TWAIN

It circulated for five years, through the halls of fifteen publishers, and finally ended up with the Vanguard Press, which, as you can see, is rather deep into the alphabet.

PATRICK DENNIS, COMMENTING
ON *AUNTIE MAME*

joy! They had *read* my story! Someone had actually read my story, not thrown it in the trash! And then they had spent a nickel to send me a postcard response! "We regret . . ." it said, so courteously.

I don't know what I expected the magazine to do—lock me in a closet, perhaps, and whip me with chains for my presumption in submitting a story.

I have also received a rejection that sent me to bed for two days, weeping, inconsolable.

⋈

A moment ago a woman telephoned whom I hardly know. She wants me to read her manuscript. Her voice lifted with false bright hopeful cheer, the kind you use to ward away rejection. She has written it eleven times, and parts are autobiographical. "It's the most important thing I've ever done in my life," she said.

I believe her, too.

⋈

In the 1980s, to show how difficult it is for a young writer to be accepted, Jerzy Kosinski resubmitted his book *Steps* under a pseudonym to several houses, including his own publisher. All of them rejected it.

⋈

In his day, the Irish writer Frank O'Connor was very well known. Some years ago, his agent, the late Cyrille Abels, told me how O'Connor was once in New York going over a story that he had sold to *The New Yorker*. On the ship back to England, he suddenly had an idea how to rewrite it, and he hardly hit his London flat before setting feverishly to work. When he had finished, however, he realized

Bringing out our little books was hard work. The great puzzle lay in the difficulty of getting answers of any kind from the publishers to whom we applied.

CHARLOTTE BRONTË

I discovered that rejections are not altogether a bad thing. They teach a writer to rely on his own judgment and to say in his heart of hearts, "To hell with you."

SAUL BELLOW

he'd forgotten the name of his editor at *The New Yorker*. "No matter," he thought; and mailed off the story with a general cover letter.

A few weeks later the story was returned with a form rejection slip.

⊗

Then there is the writer or would-be writer who wrote two or three screenplays in New York. He submitted them to producers, and received kind letters back explaining what changes he should make. He never made them. He went out drinking instead, to dull the pain of the imaginary rejections he'd received.

The opposite reaction: another friend whose novel was turned back cruelly by a major publishing house. The letter, she says, "was Kryptonite to Superman." She copied the rejection and put it above her desk as a Wall of Infamy, and every time she got discouraged "I could look up and see this letter from this sappy twenty-eight-year-old, so young she doesn't need to be a feminist, turning down my novel!"

The trick is to use the rejection to fire your intent.

And then don't throw anything away.

⊗

I find a work comes asking to be written in the form it wants. "I am a play," it calls, or "I am a novel . . . an essay, a story. . . ." Then it is up to the writer to heed the demand and be still, to listen, and to commit to what it asks of you.

Some years ago I spent four or five years writing what would become my novel *Revelations*, and when I finished the book (that draft) I sent it to my agent. In a few weeks

We have read your manuscript with boundless delight. If we were to publish your paper, it would be impossible for us to publish any work of lower standard. And as it is unthinkable that in the next thousand years we shall see its equal, we are, to our regret, compelled to return your divine composition, and to beg you a thousand times to overlook our short sight and timidity.

REJECTION SLIP FROM A CHINESE ECONOMIC
JOURNAL, QUOTED IN *THE FINANCIAL TIMES*

he returned it. "This is unmarketable," he said brutally. "Burn it. Every writer does one or two of these. You're a talented writer. Go write something I can sell."

"Unmarketable!" I was crushed. "What does that *mean?*"

His words hurt. I almost destroyed the manuscript. Then I remembered something my mother had said many years before. I don't know how she thought of it. She knew nothing of the writing business. For that matter, I don't know why it caught my attention. We were in the kitchen at the time, myself just a child of ten or twelve perhaps, with no intention of writing, when my mother suddenly turned to me.

"If you ever become a writer," she said, "remember never to throw away anything you've written. You never know when you'll want to go back and look at it again."

Now these words came curving forward across thirty years of time, as if the Universe had known all those years before that I would need to hear that song. I did not destroy the book. Instead, I put it in a box with all its various drafts. Years passed. I took a new agent. One day she asked, "Do you have anything else?"

"No. One unmarketable manuscript. But it's not worth your time to read it."

"Well, let me see it," she said; and when she had done so, "But this is *wonderful!*"

A month later she had found a publisher. In fairness to that first agent, the novel probably was unmarketable when he read it ... in that climate, at that period of time.... But times and tastes change. What is the moral? Perhaps that you never know when you'll succeed, that all you can do is to follow your path with enthusiasm, and don't let rejection get you down.

In a world where language and naming are power, silence is oppression, is violence.

ADRIENNE RICH

Creative writing is a harrowing business, a terrifying commitment to an absolute. This is it, the writer must say to himself, and I must stand or fall upon what I have put down. The degree of self-exposure is crucifying. And doubt is a constant companion. What if I am not as good as I thought? is a question that always nags, and can cripple.

WALTER KERR

✸

Sometimes rejections can stop the writing altogether. Barbara Pym had not written for years until in her late middle age she was "rediscovered" by Philip Larkin, and it makes you wonder at the writers who become well known only before they die.

✸

Some writers take classes or join with other aspiring novelists to read their work to one another and help develop their craft. It sounds ideal, but I've never been good at it. I pull back, unable to show my work until it's nearly ready for publication; that's how sensitive I am to criticism, how secretive: the fetus cannot be viewed in utero. And I am not alone. Anne Tyler shows her work to no one, unless it might be to her old teacher, Peter Taylor, until she sends it to her agent.

Once I took a class in short story writing at the New School. I was in my twenties, new to New York and to my decision to teach myself to write.

The instructor had sold nonfiction articles to *The Reader's Digest*. I don't know why he was teaching creative writing. Gamely, though, I signed up. Now, putting yourself in the hands of an Authority stirs anxiety in any heart. Each week we were to submit a story. Each week he would choose the best to read aloud and offer anonymously for discussion, and if we wished we needed never to break anonymity or claim the story's authorship.

I think it was in the second class that he chose my piece to read. I squinched down in my chair. When he finished, he looked up. "Does anyone want to comment?"

Silence. No one did.

In every real sense, the writer writes in order to teach himself, to understand himself, to satisfy himself; the publishing of his ideas is a curious anticlimax.

ALFRED KAZIN

He began, "This writer is so talented that it's a shame she—"

With a thunderous scraping of wood, I pushed back my chair, grabbed my books, and ran from the room. My heart was pounding. Tears filled my eyes. I never returned. All I heard was failure. Shame. I couldn't take the criticism.

Many times I've regretted my cowardice, wondering what he would have said. On the other hand, I know of potential writers ruined by the harshness of a teacher, the thoughtlessness, or even malice, of a fellow student. And I know of works stopped dead by showing it off too soon.

What's the solution?

Write. Read. Practice. Find a support group, if you wish. But if you want to write ... just write.

I took up magazine journalism, deciding I ought to be paid to learn the craft.

For several days after my first book was published I carried it about in my pocket, and took surreptitious peeks at it to make sure the ink had not faded.

J. M. BARRIE

Every book is the wreck of a perfect idea.

IRIS MURDOCH

You write a book and it's like putting a message in a bottle and throwing it in the ocean. You don't know if it will ever reach any shores. And there, you see, sometimes it falls in the hands of the right person.

ISABELLE ALLENDE

PUBLISHING

It took years for me to understand that the editor is on my side, that writing, like theater, is a collaborative sport. "Cut these words and they would bleed," wrote Emerson, and no writer can believe at times the stupidity of the editors he works with, or the heroic battles he will fight to keep his words intact. Again, this is a time to compliment yourself, and practice flexibility too.

It is an interesting period. You have spent hours writing words and cutting words, making corrections according to the editor's suggestions. You have read your edited manuscript and then galleys; and by now the only thing keeping your sanity is the thought that soon you will *never* have to read this book again! You see it in print, one day ... and possibly even burst into tears, as did one writer whom I know. Ashes in her mouth. "I worked all that time," she thought, "on *that!*" It suddenly seemed so small.

Now you turn businessman. The worry is getting the books in the stores and whether the publisher is promoting it, and what the advertising budget is, who will review the book—and will they? And whether even your friends will hear about it. . . .

If, however, you are one of the lucky few to have a "big" book, then your publisher will send you on a promotional tour, from city to city, and you are put up in nice

I never ask about sales. It's better not to know. I feel like I write a book, I give it to my editor, then I go back and write another one. That's what I do.

ALICE HOFFMAN

When writers die they become books, which is, after all, not too bad an incarnation.

JORGE LUIS BORGES

hotels and given a literary escort who will drive you around the unfamiliar city from radio to newspaper interview to bookstore, and you will sign copies of your books in the stores and go on radio or television talk shows; and all of this is exhilarating and exhausting and eventually horrible even to contemplate.

This is the period for "moving your book." You have six weeks to make your book a hit. You may have worked on your book for three years, five years, ten . . . and it has three months of shelf life in the stores before the new season's books come out.

It's all so discouraging, usually, that the best thing to do is go home and begin another work.

An author is a person who can never take innocent pleasure in visiting a bookstore again. Say you go in and discover that there are no copies of your book on the shelves. You resent all the other books—I don't care if they are Great Expectations, Life on the Mississippi, *and the* King James Bible—*that are on the shelves.*

ROY BLOUNT, JR.

I feel a lot of guilt about [success]. *I can also tell you it unleashes a lot of malice. You pay for your success in many ways—in other writers and other people.*

MARGARET DRABBLE

In America there seems to be an idea that writing is one big cat-and-dog fight between the various practitioners of the craft.

WILLIAM STYRON

JEALOUSY

There have been times when I could not read the *New York Times Book Review*—any book review—because my rage would build to such a peak. Joyce Carol Oates! I could feel the green dragon rise up so high I wanted to tear myself in two, like Rumpelstiltskin. I would throw the magazine across the room in jealous rage.

Tennessee Williams toward the end of his life was so jealous of the younger playwrights, like Arthur Kopit, and of the attention that his agent, Audrey Woods, paid to them—and so aware of his own declining talents—that he finally quarreled and broke with her, after twenty-five years.

It takes a world of flattery, soothing, reassurance to calm a writer's nerves. I heard that Robert Frost, at a poetry reading by Robert Lowell one evening, was so upset that he started a fire in the back of the auditorium. He couldn't stand the attention going to another poet.

Jealousy is another word for fear. Cowardice, procrastination, anxiety, hatred, inadequacy . . . I think all the dark emotions rest like fractions on a base of fear. The trick is to isolate and name it, *fear*, and then get back to work.

It's not what I do that I regret in looking back, but the things I have not dared.

Boozing does not necessarily have to go hand in hand with being a writer, as seems to be the concept in America. I therefore solemnly declare to all young men trying to become writers that they do not actually have to become drunkards first.

NELSON W. ALDRICH, JR.

No one, ever, wrote anything as well even after one drink as he would have done without it.

RING LARDNER

Alcohol doesn't console, it doesn't fill up anyone's psychological gaps; all it replaces is the lack of God.

MARGUERITE DURAS

ALCOHOL,
DRUGS,
DEPRESSION,
SUICIDE

So hard is writing, this creative endeavor, so much at the mercy of loneliness, rejection, stress, or that horrible feeling of being "blocked," that the seduction of drink or drugs is nearly irresistible; for, as critic Alfred Kazin put it, alcohol, the lubricant, "cuts the connections that keep us anxious." At first it oils the grinding friction of writing. Then it becomes a pleasure independent of its effects. Later it disconnects our critical faculties and blurs the mind, and later still it starts to feed on us.

I am afraid of drugs—booze and cocaine, pot, heroin, even caffeine. I remember once when I was young writing with a glass of cognac by my typewriter and thinking as I watched with pleasure the glorious golden color in the glass, "Now I'm a *real* writer. . . ." The thought scared me. I don't have enough brain cells to give away any to drugs,

But suicide, quick or slow, a sudden spill or a gradual oozing away through the years is the price John Barleycorn exacts. No friend of his ever escapes making the just, due payment.

JACK LONDON

I should like to sit down with 1/2 dozen chosen companions and drink myself to death but I am sick alike of life, liquor and literature.

F. SCOTT FITZGERALD

I have spent my life straightening out rummies and all my life drinking, but since writing is my true love I never get the two things mixed up.

ERNEST HEMINGWAY

and looking at the history of the writers in the last century I recoil in dismay. Five of the six American Nobel Prize winners in literature were lushes—William Faulkner, Sinclair Lewis, Eugene O'Neill, Ernest Hemingway, John Steinbeck.

According to a study at Washington University in Saint Louis, one-third to one-half of the well-known American writers from the last hundred years were alcoholics. (Of course the same might be said about half the housepainters, but it's writing that concerns me, and the stimulants that form the writers' curse.)

Listen to this list: Edgar Allan Poe, Hart Crane, Conrad Aiken, Edna St. Vincent Millay, Thomas Wolfe, Dorothy Parker, James Jones, Dashiell Hammett, James Agee, Malcolm Lowry, John Cheever, Jack Kerouac, John O'Hara, Dylan Thomas, Raymond Carver . . . We're not even talking about the opium-eaters of the last century, the dreams of Coleridge, the destruction of Quincey or Branwell Brontë.

F. Scott Fitzgerald died an alcoholic at forty-four, Ring Lardner at forty-eight, Brendan Behan at forty-one. Tennessee Williams, who fell into the hands of a drug-dispensing therapist, became so paranoid under drugs that he accused people of putting ground glass in his vodka. Hemingway by mid-life was downing two fifths of Scotch a day, and losing his mind, his ability to eat, have sex or write. In 1961, at the age of only sixty-one, he took a shotgun and blew out his brains. Dorothy Parker, binging and sobering up, agreed at a party once to collaborate with a young writer, and next day did not remember either his face or name.

If not alcohol, then drugs. Eugene O'Neill gave up alcohol in his thirties and later became addicted to sleeping

I never try to write a line when I'm not strictly on the wagon.
EUGENE O'NEILL

I have felt the wind of the wing of madness.
CHARLES BAUDELAIRE

No more words. An act. I'll never write again.
CESARE PAVESE

pills. Jack London, who at forty deliberately overdosed on morphine, regularly took morphine, belladonna, heroin, and strychnine—which might explain his manic working hours, if not his suicide.

⊗

Depression: Winston Churchill called it the "Black Dog," and William Styron the "gathering murk." Styron, himself a victim of this horrible illness, writes in *Darkness Visible* that as many as one in ten Americans suffer depression, but that artists—and poets in particular—seem especially vulnerable, as if the brain cells, overworked, collapse like a camel dropping to its knees. Depression sometimes leads to suicide. Among the writers Styron names are Virginia Woolf, Romain Gary, Arshile Gorky, Randall Jarrell, Primo Levi (who lived through Auschwitz only to throw himself down a Turin staircase in 1987 at the age of sixty-seven), Sylvia Plath, Vachel Lindsay, John Berryman, Anne Sexton.

⊗

Styron was hospitalized to get free of the drugs that induced his agony, and being a writer, he immediately set out to record his journey through hell. Having recovered, he quotes the hopeful final line of Dante's *Inferno*: "And so we came forth, and once again beheld the stars."

(Much as I like Styron, I dislike his translation, and cannot keep myself from impatiently rewriting it to: "And so we came forth, to see the stars again.")

⊗

I guard my emotions. I watch for signs of melancholia, and watch what I pour into my body, too—no alcohol, drugs,

Bad readers have asked me if I was drugged when I wrote some of my works. But that illustrates that they don't know anything about literature or drugs. To be a good writer you have to be absolutely lucid at every moment of writing, and in good health.

GABRIEL GARCÍA MÁRQUEZ

caffeine. I have become so sensitive to my body's claims that now I actually often eat when hungry (imagine!), stop and lie down when tired. It has taken me years to learn to listen for those two simple demands, knowing that I write better when the machinery's warmed up, oiled, clean.

It's as hard to get from almost finished to finished as to get from beginning to almost done.

ELINOR FUCHS

The qualities that make a true artist [are] nearly the same qualities that make a true athlete.

JOHN GARDNER

Writer's
Block

And now we come to what every writer shrinks from: writer's block.

And I stop. Blocked.

I do not like this subject. I came to this section and put the work aside. I couldn't bear to look at it. As if in contemplating block, it might rub off on me, an infectious disease.

Block is different from a dry period, when the writer has nothing to say. Block means sitting before a project that you know you want to create and being unable to find the words. Your hand stops. Your mind recoils. It is then that you are tempted to turn to drugs and drink, which may also cause a block.

⌘

I sometimes think block is caused by loss of concentration, which is a signal of lack of faith. The ego lifts its eye to the future to gauge the effect the work will have (to Sell! to Sell!) and in that glance of desire, that movement toward the fruits of the labor—publication, validation, money, fame, or conversely, the fear that none of these

In order to get in touch I have to block out ego. Ego is the piece of me that's going, How am I doing, champ? . . . So you like this? . . . Because that has nothing to do with creating. That has to do with the finished work that's out in the world and that's a very separate creature. So I need to work from within. . . . Not thinking anything. Not making judgments about myself. Not sitting critiquing myself but being still enough to hear the voice that'll tell me what I'm supposed to do next.

SUE GRAFTON

will come—in that moment, the creative self loses its way and is paralyzed by doubt.

But block is also caused sometimes by the Inner Judge, with its sharp, critical faculties coming in too early to do its work. A time will come for this harsh, demanding inner critic—later, during the editing period, but not while you are freshly putting words on paper. Frederich von Schiller said it best, when he wrote in 1788 to a friend who was complaining of writer's block:

> The ground for your complaint seems to me to lie in the constraint imposed by your reason upon your imagination. I will make my idea more concrete by a simile. It seems a bad thing and detrimental to the creative work of the mind if Reason makes too close an examination of the ideas as they come pouring in—at the very gateway as it were. Looked at in isolation, a thought may seem very trivial or very fantastic: but it may be made important by another thought that comes after it, and in conjunction with other thoughts, that may seem equally absurd, it may turn out to form a most effective link. Reason cannot form any opinion upon all this unless it retains the thought long enough to look at it in connection with the others. On the other hand, where there is a creative mind, Reason—so it seems to me—relaxes its watch upon the gates and the ideas rush in pell-mell, and only then does it look them through and examine them in a mass. You critics, or whatever else you may call yourself, are ashamed or frightened of the momentary and transient extravagances which are to be found in all truly creative

You notice only this: your worker—your one and only, your prized, coddled, and driven worker—is not going out on that job. Will not budge, not even for you boss. Has been at it long enough to know when the air smells wrong; can sense a tremor through boot soles. Nonsense, you say; it is perfectly safe. But the worker will not go. Will not even look at the site. Just developed heart trouble. Would rather starve. Sorry.

ANNIE DILLARD

Borges said we go on writing the same story all our lives. The trouble is, it's usually a story that can never be told.

ROBERT COOVER

minds and whose longer or shorter duration distinguishes the thinking artist from the dreamer. You complain of your unfruitfulness because you reject too soon and discriminate too severely.

⊗

Sometimes writer's block is caused by unfinished efforts regarding the work. You haven't let the material simmer long enough; you're afraid to let it cook. You must back off and let it steam.

Sometimes it comes from attacking the problem from the wrong direction. You are about to make a mistake. You are stumped. The book wants to take a fork, and you don't dare let it. You won't give up and see where it wants to go.

⊗

Sometimes when you land on writer's block, you simply back off, stop work and go get exercise—physically exhausting exercise—for that day or even for several weeks. Or you try a change of scenery, country, culture to jog the mind. Or else you do right-brain repatterning exercises, to balance an overstimulated brain.

Drawing or painting—changing your creative gears—may help.

⊗

Sometimes the block will pass by itself, mysteriously, slouching off as silently as it came, and you will never know why it appeared . . . or why it slogged away.

⊗

Sometimes it comes from fear of failure, stress or depression.

What happens when a writer doesn't want to write anymore?
When the progression of fingers across the keyboard is like an
old dry horse hitched to the millstone, blinders and yoke lashed,
the only path between day and nightfall one's own scoured rut
of circling footsteps?

RITA DOVE

If the doors of perception were cleansed, everything would ap-
pear to man as it is, infinite.

WILLIAM BLAKE

Sometimes it comes from too tight a hold on your imagination. Then you must write something more extravagant. Outlandish. Preposterous. Wild. Break through your own inhibitions and play and dance and sing and shout your verses to the moon. Or else you stop writing what is giving you such trouble and write about the writing that you hate, or the subject that wants to be turned upside down and poured out like stars into the heavens, a Milky Way of nonsense that the creative sense adores.

⊗

Sometimes you don't know what it's from. And then you must hold your anguish in your arms and rock yourself to sleep with lullabies that soothe the starved, abandoned, and neglected heart. I remember once discussing with a playwright how we talked to ourselves when we're not working well. "Oh, I speak roughly to myself!" I said. "I scold myself and shout and whip at myself to quit this laziness and get to work. It's only WEAKNESS!" I tell myself, "Get up and MOVE!"

She looked at me in surprise. "Oh, no," she said. "You must never speak to yourself like that, and especially when you're feeling bad. No, what you do is to put your arm around your shoulder and comfort yourself and talk baby talk to yourself, and give yourself a present, and hold your frightened self. . . ." I was amazed. I'd never heard of that. But the next time I felt despairing I remembered her advice—and to my surprise my heart immediately lifted, and immediately I sat back down to work.

⊗

In *The New Yorker*, Norman Rush tells John Leonard's story of how the late Japanese novelist Kobo Abe fell into

My *vocation has always rejected me; it does not want to know about me. . . . This vocation is a master who is able to beat us till the blood flows, a master who reviles and condemns us.*

NATALIA GINZBURG

The most beautiful thing we can experience is the mysterious. It is the source of all true art and science.

ALBERT EINSTEIN

a depression and severe writer's block after reading Gabriel García Márquez's *One Hundred Years of Solitude*. He could not write for years. Leonard kept in touch with Abe and later he learned that when Márquez won the Nobel Prize, Abe could write again. Abe's wife explained that Márquez being "among the immortals now, there need no longer be any question of competition."

∞

I have learned in recent years that my faults, the defects that keep me from creating the work I want to do, are not flaws or failures. They are wounds. The merest shift in word shifts attitude. As *failures, flaws, defects*, I want to crush them underfoot, smash their noses in, impale their heads upon a pike and mount it on the tower wall. But this is my very soul I am impaling there, the essence of my heart. Block, the inability to proceed, signals not a defect but a wound exposed; and curiously in our wounds lie our divinity. This is too large a subject to take up, and I shall drop it here, except to add that healing comes from tenderness. Embrace the wounds, wash them, bandage them with loving care. . . .

Is the defect an overly developed sense of perfectionism or fear of failure? Then I must acknowledge the underlying cause, the desire to succeed; I hold it gently until, feeling safe, it can push its fragile head above the earth again and sprout a leaf. . . . Is the defect pride? Or arrogance? Then let me notice the contrary need for recognition and give myself some praise, until my feelings of lack or scarcity have diminished and been replaced by humble gratitude.

∞

"Yes," I said, suddenly becoming serious. "I am very lucky, but I have a little theory about this. I have noticed through experience and through my own observations that Providence, Nature, God, or what I would call the Power of Creation seems to favor human beings who accept and love life unconditionally. And I am certainly one who does, with all my heart. So I have discovered as a result of what I can only call miracles that whenever my inner self desires something subconsciously, life will somehow grant it to me."

ARTHUR RUBINSTEIN

What to do about writer's block?

Write anyway • play a game • do a monotonous dirty task • take a walk • get a job • wait • pray • talk to friends • paint • listen to music • be confident • go into analysis • move to a new city • or country • read • abandon all desire • write something else • do more research • give up all drugs and drinking for a year • "waste" your talents by producing more and more in a genius of abundance • enjoy • write letters to your children • release yourself from all judgment, including the idea that you ever have to write again anything at all. . . .

Do all these things at once, joyfully and with gratitude, because for a moment you have been given a respite from your work. The creative obsession will fall on you again, after this period of incubation. And if it does not, you tell yourself cavalierly, so what? Then you begin work anyway.

⚘

Reynolds Price, author of more than twenty novels, plays, memoirs, and biblical translations, says he has never been seriously blocked, except immediately after his first surgery for spinal cancer, followed by five weeks of radiation. For about five months he sat in a chair gazing out the window, unable to read, unable to write. It was a "spiritual hunkering down," he says, as he concentrated his resources on getting well.

So sometimes a writer's block serves as a healer, too. I've hardly heard of a writer who is not at some time paralyzed. My block came as my husband and I were splitting up, and for a year, while I entered therapy, I had no energy to write.

⚘

Nothing in the world can take the place of Persistence. Talent will not; nothing is more common than unsuccessful men with talent. Genius will not; unrewarded genius is almost a proverb. Education alone will not; the world is full of educated derelicts. Persistence and determination alone are omnipotent.

ANONYMOUS

The prolific poet Frank O'Hara described his one bout with writer's block. He was trying to write in a borrowed apartment, in vain, until he put up favorite pictures and photos on the wall.

❋

I mention prayer as one release for writer's block. I mean, you pray with trust. Abandon your failure, this blocked flow, to your higher center, the Source, this loving Creator whose mercy and joy belie all understanding. You throw yourself upon the mercy of the Universe. Accept the fact: you're blocked. Don't fight; and without panic but only a detached observance, go ask for help, concerning this problem, *of* this problem, which may be your friend. "What do you want to tell me?" you ask it, and you pour love upon this wound or the message being sent to you. You bless its coming to guide you where you are supposed to go. And then you go to work and sit and wait, and you exercise, and enjoy, and talk to other writers patiently, doing all the things that are mentioned above.

Essentially I think that writing is a spiritual release. It can never be the result of pressure. Writing is a fiery practice, a full engagement, but for me it comes with the acknowledgment—and leads to the acknowledgement—of the sacredness of all life, all living breathing spaces both in and outside us, and of worship of this space. Paradoxically, this sacredness includes the blocks that indicate a pause, a bleeding sore, a lack of confidence.

❋

Go smaller. Often you experience block by taking too big a bite. You look up in panic at the prospect of swallowing the entire elephant of your plan . . . and choke. Now is

Until one is committed there is hesitancy, the chance to draw back, always ineffectiveness. Concerning all acts of initiative (and creation) there is one elementary truth, the ignorance of which kills countless ideas and splendid plans; that the moment one definitely commits oneself, then Providence moves too. All sorts of things occur to one that would never otherwise have occurred. A whole stream of events issue from the decision, raising in one's favor all manner of unforeseen incidents and meetings and material assistance, which no man could have dreamt would have come his way.

E . H . M U R R A Y

the time to focus your attention on the small and smaller and with Buddhist mindfulness still smaller yet, onto the tiniest, most intimate detail—not on the branching trees against the sky, but on one leaf or smaller still upon the tracery of one capillary of its veins. "Today," you tell your-self, "I will write only that one short paragraph about the ankles of the ant...." And always you give thanks and praises to your ability to write. Small bites. It is surprising how much gets eaten, taking one small forkful at a time.

Surreptitiously, then, you fight, and one day you re-member that writing, creating art, erupts from enthusiasm. The word means "possessed by God," and brings with it happiness, which is William James's definition of sanity and health. I add love, remembering Sigmund Freud's comment that there is only love and illness, and if you do not love you will get ill. In happiness you must create. You cannot help it: you knit, cook, make gardens, patch up hurt animals, build companies, make valentines with the children, carve wood; but you create. It is part of your spirit. You play music, you dance, you move your body in an exuberance of joy—running, sailing, walking, skiing, swimming, the movement itself a hymn of praise to being alive. And if you cannot move, you create anyway: I think of the paraplegics who hold a brush in their mouths to paint. Unstoppable!

⚭

Sometimes writer's block is no more than a signal that you have not done enough research. The unconscious stops dead, balking like a good horse that's terrified of stepping on an unsafe bridge. In that case, then, you delve more deeply into the subject, do more interviewing, more read-ing, more thinking to build a solid structure; until one day

Ever tried? Ever failed? No matter. Try again. Fail again. Fail better.

SAMUEL BECKETT

Whatever you can do or dream you can, begin it;
Boldness has genius, power and magic in it.

JOHANN WOLFGANG GOETHE

you find the horse's ears pricking forward, and then it takes a tentative step without a whip or spur and then another and soon you find it breaking into a trot. Halloo! You are writing again.

No matter how hard he tries to put it off, the true writer cannot stop. One day the urge creeps up on him. He must begin again.

He is ready to write, he is fully equipped. His fountain pen is comfortably full, the house is quiet, the tobacco and the matches are together, the night is young and we shall leave him in this pleasurable situation and gently steal out, and close the door, firmly push out of the house, as we go, the monster of grim commonsense that is lumbering up the step to whine that the book is not for the general public, that the book will never, never—and right then, just before it blurts out the word s, e, double-l, false commonsense must be shot dead.

VLADIMIR NABOKOV

CLOSING
THE
CIRCLE

My friend from California, John Sack, went home after our visit. I heard nothing from him until a few months later, when he informed me that he had taken a job with a local television network. He was writing for the national news, and was happy to be doing so, content to be with people again and lick the wounds of isolation. But we both knew—as if hearing a musical overtone trembling in the air—that in a while he would get the itch again, a wanderlust, to be off on his own in his room engaged in the struggle with another book, or another play, or another film.

When that happens all the emotions of writing will rush over him again: anguish, despair, delight, or manic joy at what he is writing, horror at the banality of his words, and then, finally, a sense of awe and gratitude. A ringing, deep humility when the words are flowing forth,

Writing is a lonely life, but the only life worth living.

GUSTAVE FLAUBERT

when the Muse arrives and sweeps him up in her arms, away on a river of good words. Then he knows there is nothing finer he could have in life, nothing more that anyone could want.

As soon as you trust yourself you will know how to live.

JOHANN WOLFGANG GOETHE

AFTERWORD

The scraps of years of gossip, reading, and observation have gone into this patchwork quilt about my craft; biographies and autobiographies, snippets from book reviews, and the quotations collected by myself or passed on to me by editors and friends.

Two of the many books from which I took these stories or quotations were so helpful—and so fascinating—that I particularly want to acknowledge them. One is *The Gift: Imagination and the Erotic Life of Property* (Vintage, 1983) by Lewis Hyde, and the other is a treasure I found remaindered: *Novels and Novelists. A Guide to the World of Fiction*, edited by Martin Seymour-Smith (St. Martin's Press, 1980). And lucky the person who finds either one.

But look also to the *Paris Review* interviews with writers that go back decades, and to writers' journals and—manna for us starving writers—writers writing on their craft: John Gardner, Annie Dillard, Naomi Epel, Julia Cameron, Eudora Welty. . . . There are dozens of these books. Some stories came from conversations with friends, and a few from personal interviews.

As for quotations, they are easy to find; but one valuable source came in the form of a chapter photocopied and sent to me, "What the Masters Know," from the book

Resources for the Teacher of Writing. A search reveals nothing about this book—publisher, author, date.

Many people helped with *For Writers Only*, knowingly or unknowingly, but I remember especially my beloved friend Jane Vonnegut Yarmolinsky, who before her death delighted in an early draft and thereby encouraged its completion. I wish to thank Susanne Nicolson, Sarah Flynn, and David Laskin, who all helped in later drafts; and, with special warmth, my agent and friend Anne Edelstein, my editor Joëlle Delbourgo, and finally the forgotten ones in publishing: all the salesmen and booksellers who read and love books and their authors, and through whose caring hands our words and hopes go forth.

❈

SOPHY BURNHAM has distinguished herself as a novelist, journalist, nonfiction writer, and playwright. Her nonfiction credits include the bestselling *A Book of Angels* and *Angel Letters*, as well as *The Landed Gentry*, and her *New York Times* bestseller, *The Art Crowd*. She is also the author of two novels, *Revelations* and *The President's Angel*. Currently Executive Director of the Fund for New American Plays, she has written award-winning theater plays, radio plays, and documentary films. Ms. Burnham's journalism has appeared frequently in national magazines, including *Esquire*, *New York*, *The New York Times Sunday Magazine*, *Town & Country*, and *New Woman*.